*What Others a**e Sa*ing *about
Meditations for Women*

"I can't tell you what a marvelous feeling I get when I read my daily meditation. I feel so fortunate to have discovered you. I have told many others about its incredibly empowering and healing benefits!!! Thank you so much for providing such beauty and hope to each day; your messages are truly gifts."
    -Maria

"I just love these meditations. It feels like no matter how I am feeling or hurdle I am dealing with, the daily meditations talk exactly to what is going on with me. I want to thank you for these great inspirational readings. They help me SO much."
    -Lorrinda

"I do NOT believe that I could obtain any more self-worth from a psychiatrist then what YOU give me each and every time I read your messages. They may be brief…but oh-so-powerful."
    -Daveen

"Thank you for the daily meditations. I am a recovering addict; these meditations give me some extra strength every day. God bless you for sharing your experience, strength and hope."
    -Sharon

"I truly enjoy daily meditations for women. The ideas are thought-provoking, substantial and inspiring. Thank you!"
    -Bonnie

"I am a subscriber to your daily meditations and they are superbbbbbb. They have been my biggest source of inspiration through very testing times."   -Kris

"I got up this morning, feeling glum and depressed. I read today's meditation - it was perfect. I'm feeling much more positive and hopeful."   -Jackie

"Words cannot express my gratitude for your daily meditations. I often used to feel down and had very low self-esteem, but reading your meditations has really given me a different outlook on life. Your words have enlightened me in so many ways. No more negativity, no more low self-esteem, no more fear. Thank you so much for literally changing my life."   -Denise

"I can't begin my day without reading the meditation. I have put all my friends on to you and each day we have a little chat about what we have read."   -Rachel

"I cannot even begin to express my gratitude. I'm a radio host and I have a little way I close my show, it's called "The Final Thought." Your meditations have inspired at least 50% of my closing thoughts. Thank you so much!"   -Alex

"I would just like, to say THANK YOU for your meditations. I suffer from major depression and Post Traumatic Stress Disorder and appreciate each and every one of your meditations. They have made such a difference and helped me immensely get through a difficult time."   −Ava

"I (at times), like many women, use my relationship to define my happiness. I have been trying very hard over the past 2 years to allow myself to think otherwise - not the easiest task. Your meditations have truly made a difference for me. Thank you for starting my day with a reminder that I'm okay just as me!!!"
        -Debbie

Meditations for Women

Jane Powell

High Sierra Publishing
Olympic Valley, California

Meditations for Women
Jane Powell
High Sierra Publishing
P.O. Box 2335
Olympic Valley, CA 96146
http://www.meditationsforwomen.com

ISBN-13: 978-0-9799977-0-9
ISBN-10: 0-9799977-0-4

Printed and bound in the
United States of America
CA 10 9 8 7 6 5 4 3 2 1

"You must create the space in your life to enable your inner guide to share her wisdom, her creativity, her courage. Unleashed, she is the single most potent resource you have."
-Marilyn O. Sifford

January

January 1

"Strengthening your mind is like strengthening your body - it takes time."

Outer strength takes persistence, time and a commitment to regular exercise. Inner strength requires exactly the same thing. It won't happen overnight but once you start, you'll notice you're feeling a little stronger inside, day by day.

Exercise every aspect of your mind on a regular basis. Exercise your courage and sense of adventure by seizing new experiences. Exercise your patience and wisdom by taking time to think things through. Exercise your determination, persistence and commitment to self-improvement by deciding that no matter how long it takes, you're going to become a stronger woman - starting today!

January 2

"You are your own best judge."

When you start judging yourself by looking through the eyes of your parents, husband, friends or boss, you end up running around doing more and more in an effort to gain their approval. It does not take long before you end up feeling exhausted, resentful and ready to give up.

Trying to live your life by the expectations of others disconnects you from your own desires. It leaves you feeling empty and unmotivated. The gratification that comes from fulfilling the expectations of others is very little and short-lived.

Reclaim the energy and happiness that is rightfully yours! Be your own judge and live by your own expectations. As you reclaim your potential, you will thrive and feel energized, because you are accomplishing things that are important to you. Start today!

January 3

"Proactive women make success, health, happiness and wealth happen."

Proactive women have a certain mind-set, which includes big dreams, good habits, imagination, strong positive beliefs and unshakable inner confidence. These women don't just "talk the talk, "they "walk the talk."

Such women love and embrace the adventures of life. They attract opportunities, good people and harmonious situations that reflect the same mind-set. They are passionate and feel the joy in whatever they do.

The only thing standing between you and women like this is your mind. Right now, make a conscious decision to get in the habit of feeling prosperous, happy, grateful, accepted, healthy, loved and successful. Amazing things will happen as you open your mind to possibilities!

January 4

"Finding balance is the key to personal fulfillment."

If your life was a symphony, all the different parts of it could be represented by the different sections of the orchestra. All the parts would work together to produce beautiful harmonies. Not one section would conflict with the other.

Too often we think in terms of conflicts rather than complements, as though the different roles we play are at odds with one another. We struggle with having a successful career and a fulfilling family life.

Dissolve this conflict and begin to assess your life as a whole with complementary parts, rather than broken fragments competing for your time and attention. Ultimately balance will come from living in full of awareness of yourself not the parts.

January 5

"Confidence comes from your internal power plant."

Confidence is a strong, powerful force. When it is part of your heart, you have the ability to conquer any obstacles life may throw at you.

Undoubtedly, situations will come up where you may feel uncertain or less confident. Don't let doubtful feelings stop you. It's up to you and nobody else to keep going in times of uncertainty.

There is a saying, "Fake it till you make it." You can pretend to be what you want to be until you grow into it. Try it. It's what a lot of successful women admit to doing when they are unsure.

It doesn't take long before the power of your confidence resurfaces and you're back on track to achieving your goals.

January 6

"Ahhh, soothe, reassure and relax."

Each woman needs a regime for recharging and relaxing. Ask yourself, "What makes me most comfortable?" "What soothes me?" "What recharges me?"

It can be as simple as a bubble bath or lighting candles. How about a long walk or a phone call to a good friend? Perhaps a nap, a massage or a shopping spree is in your future?

Make a list of your rechargers, relaxers and soothers. Include in your list ones that you can do on short notice like sitting down with a cup of your favorite tea or watching a favorite movie classic. Put your list somewhere where you will see it and be reminded by it.

Next, do something on your list at least once a week. It will clear your mind put things in perspective and ultimately put you in charge of you. And, one last thing don't feel guilty for taking time for you.

January 7

"Formalize your commitment and you'll see results."

An excellent way to formalize your goals and commitments is by writing a contract to yourself. Spell out clearly and precisely as you can what your goals are. Include step-by-step details of how and when you are going to achieve them. Sign and date your contract. Next share it with someone you trust and post it where you will see it and be reminded by it. And, as with all contracts, stick to the obligations.

Don't forget to include in your contract how you are going to reward yourself for your accomplishments. You have made a deal with yourself. You have worked hard and when you're done you deserve a reward.

January 8

"You hold your future in your mind."

Let your mind flow freely for a moment. Look into the future and imagine that you have no limitations on what you can be, have or do. Imagine that you have everything you need to get there. Time, money, people, smarts are all readily available.

What do you see?

Your future vision is an imaginary creation of your ideal life and this vision flows from your most important values. It idealizes both who you are and who you can become.

Let your vision crystallize so clearly that you can almost touch it. Let yourself feel the emotion that comes with imaging your ideal life. Once you do, you'll be amazed by the energy it brings.

The steps you need to take to turn your vision into reality will crystallize, too. This is your pathway to an ideal future.

January 9

"The best decisions are made with self-awareness."

Decisions. You face them every day. It's the big ones that are tough. First and foremost, when facing a big decision, you have to know what is important to you. It may sound selfish, but it's not. It is essential to making the best possible choices.

Avoid making decisions because someone else is pressuring you. You may start out with the best intentions but you won't be motivated to carry through and you may often live with regret.

Next time you're faced with a big decision, take the time to examine your own thoughts and beliefs. Your feelings, ideas and experiences are what you must think about before making a big commitment.

Self-awareness is the key to how the best decisions are made.

January 10

"People respect you as much as you respect yourself."

Ever wonder what it is about some women that commands respect? Is it the way they walk? Perhaps it's the way they talk? Or maybe it is the way they dress? Some of this may be true, but the real secret to respect is having respect for yourself.

Self-respect is about self-confidence, self-affirmation and self-caring. Be proud of what you do, who you are, what you stand for, where you come from and where you're going.

When you practice self-respect two things happen. You're less tolerant of disrespect from others and you set an example of how you expect to be treated.

Try it, you'll get amazing results!

January 11

"Have you neglected your potential lately?"

Your potential is the part of you that seeks your best self. It is the part of you that aspires to learn and grow as a woman. Your potential shines when you find fulfillment in what you do best.

What may be fulfilling for you may not be for others. For you it may be poetry, gardening or cooking. For someone else it may be fitness or music, etc. Take an inventory of your gifts, talents and abilities. What makes your heart sing?

Your satisfaction, motivation and peace of mind in life are all tied to meeting your potential.

If you have been neglecting your potential, you know what to do!

January 12

"A positive attitude is within your reach."

There will be times when you find yourself in situations that seem impossible to deal with. Maybe you are in one now. Perhaps you're in a dead end job or a relationship that seems to be going nowhere. Maybe your family is driving you crazy.

Whatever your situation, remember, many women have stood in your shoes. They found a way to overcome obstacles and solve problems. But, how did they do it? They figured out a way to keep a positive attitude through the hardest of times. They did not focus on the gloom, but on the resolutions. If they could do it, so can you.

A positive attitude is yours for the making. Grab it now and turn those bad situations into mere bumps in the road of life.

January 13

"Stretch and take a deep breath..."

Do you spend a lot of time feeling anxious and stressed? Does your body have its own way of tightening? Do your shoulders feel tense and hard? Maintaining this state for periods of time can do all kinds of unpleasant things to your mind and your body.

It's essential that you relax and take care of yourself. Here's how. Have you ever watched a sleeping baby? Babies breathe in and out, with their tummy muscles. As adults, we hold our tummies in, focused on that perfect figure. But, breathing slowly, from your tummy, is the first step to total relaxation.

With that in mind, try this simple escape. Find a comfortable chair in a quiet place and just breathe, in and out, like a sleeping baby or a confident adult. Tune into the rhythm of your breathing. Shun away other thoughts. Within minutes your shoulders will relax, the anxiousness will subside and you will feel the stress leave your body. And, all you had to do was breathe like a baby.

Feels pretty good, doesn't it?

January 14

"The easiest kind of relationship is with many; the hardest is with just one."

Many of us feel less vulnerable when we're with a group of people. No one's looking at us closely and no one knows us intimately. It's easy to hide our real nature along with our true feelings.

In truth, however, "easy" isn't always best. When you open yourself up and share honest feelings one-on-one with someone, you stand to gain the rewards of a rich and lasting bond that could never be formed with a group.

Yes, one-on-one relationships are more work, but when you treasure these relationships and work to maintain them, the emotional rewards are priceless.

January 15

"When you let go of things, they let go of you."

When you harbor resentment, anger or bitterness, the person you end up harming the most is yourself. Negative emotions have a way of creating negative energy that destroys positive emotions, like generosity, love and joy. Although the unhappy situation may be long gone, you may be allowing it to hold you back by holding onto the feelings it evoked.

Today, vow to start "cleaning out" that inner vault of negativism. Try to forgive those who've caused you previous pain and if you can't forgive, at least learn to forget.

Break free! Let go! Move forward with optimism. It's the best way to find happiness.

January 16

"Inner strength is just a decision away."

You probably can think of someone whom you admire and respect. Perhaps you admire her ambition to learn new skills. Maybe it is her perseverance to overcome difficulties and hardships. Why can't that person be you?

It can and the key is willpower and self-discipline. You have it in you even if you refuse to believe it.

Each one of us is confronted and tempted by an endless stream of temptations; many of which aren't that important. When you learn to refuse to satisfy all of them, and choose only to satisfy those that are in line with your priorities you sharpen your willpower and strengthen your self-discipline.

Try it. You'll quickly become the woman to admire!

January 17

"Do you lack motivation?"

D oes it grow tougher to quit smoking, to start that diet, to workout, get projects done or follow through on goals and decisions? If so, it's time to evaluate your self-motivation.

Motivation through negative self-talk, like, "I am so fat, what's the point in dieting," "I have to do this whether I like it or not" or "I will never be loved until I've reached this goal" may get you started, but it won't sustain you in the long run.

Motivation for the long haul comes when you learn to truly appreciate what you have already accomplished and value your previous successes. When you embrace this frame of mind, you'll find you're internally motivated to accomplish more. And, that can change motivation into accomplishment!

January 18

"Why is it we never notice what has been done, but only what remains to be done?"

W e do it as mothers when we focus on the one messy shelf in child's bedroom, not the four that are tidy and neat. We do it in the workplace when we leap to point out what hasn't been finished, instead of commenting on progress made. We do it to ourselves when we focus on goals not met, instead of on success achieved.

It's this negative point of view that will bring you down and reduce your motivation. Not the best way to achieve new goals!

Starting today, resolve to be more positive! Look for what has been done; not for what's left undone. Praise children, colleagues, friends and partners for efforts and progress. Concentrate on your own achievements. The more you recognize and appreciate success, the more success will follow!

January 19

"Self-confidence is an attitude."

Got a pear shape instead of an hourglass figure? Born with two left feet? Some things we can't do much about, but some things we can. Self-confidence is among the latter, thank goodness!

Self-confidence isn't about becoming something you're not, but about recognizing what you already are. Every day, think about the things that make you special; celebrate your skills and your personality attributes; feel proud and walk with your head held high. Before you know it, you'll be able to add self-confidence to your list of the things that make you YOU!

January 20

"Allow yourself comfort and joy."

Think about everything you've done for other people this week; the ways you brought comfort and joy to partners, children, parents and friends. Now think about the things you did for yourself. Chances are, there's a big imbalance, right?

As women, we need to remember to nurture our own emotional needs and make our well being a priority. Give yourself permission to feel tired or sad. Comfort yourself with a leisurely bath or an early night with a great book. Stay connected with others and seek joy through a lunch with friends. Why not treat yourself to a bouquet of your favorite flowers? There are so many things you can do.

It's important that you comfort yourself so you have the energy to take care of others without resentment. Through this you feel comfort and joy!

January 21

"Take pride and joy as a mother, you deserve it."

If you are a mother or even a mentor take notice of the successes of everyday life that occur by just being who you are.

Perhaps your child is faced with a decision, rather than stepping in you watch and wait to see how she uses her judgment. You watch her take the time to think it through and come to a decision.

You as a mother should feel proud. You are the one who taught her the importance of making good decisions. You are the one who taught her to have the confidence to know that she could think it through and make a choice.

As a parent, you did it by just being who you are and you should be proud.

January 22

"Have you reached your destination?"

Many of us grow up not knowing what we want to do with our lives. It can take years to figure it out, and some never do. Many women change jobs, careers and husbands, searching for their purpose and destination.

To achieve success in finding your way, soul-searching is a necessity. Have an honest conversation with yourself and answer a very tough question. "Who am I?" Think about your strengths, your weaknesses and most importantly your passions.

It may take a day, a week or a month but, when you answer this question, your personal destination becomes clear.

Your direction will not fall in your lap, so don't waste another moment – create an inner compass and find it yourself.

January 23

"Challenges add riches to the journey of life."

There's not a single woman in the world that hasn't had to struggle with something or overcome difficulties. At some point we all face challenges and even discouragement. You may be facing them at this very moment, whether they're related to money, health, children, lovers, family or careers. It's all part of life.

Recognize that obstacles are a wonderful part of life's journey. They can enrich rather than paralyze you. When you see obstacles as milestones, they both measure your progress and increase your strength. Each challenge, successfully overcome, brings you closer your goals and potential.

Remember, with every challenge passed, you're a little stronger, a little wiser and a whole lot more experienced.

January 24

"Confidence is sexy."

Think about what you find attractive in others and chances are that looks are not number one on your list. Self-confidence is their most attractive feature. In fact, confidence is not only attractive, it's downright irresistible!

Let's face it - that's great news!

It means you can be sexy without spending a fortune on designer wardrobes or expensive hairdressers. All you need is confidence, which is available without a price tag.

It's something that shines from within when you believe in yourself. And its glow shines brighter than diamonds in your eyes and in your smile.

Show the world how hopeful and confident you are about your life and your future. You'll be sexy without even trying!

January 25

"It all starts with a vision."

A vision is an inspired idea. It is a concept that motivates you and pushes you into action.

You know when a vision hits you, by the energy and excitement you feel. A clear vision gets you charged and keeps you going. The very thought fills you with energy and positive feelings.

Your visions inspire a sense of purpose and direction. They give you a target to aim for, an aspiration to live for. With the motivation that comes from visions, you can transform yourself and your life.

Once you have a vision in mind, use the energy it inspires to create a plan. Then, imagine the plan in motion and the vision achieved. That's how visions become realities!

January 26

"Increase the quality of your being through fitness."

Although we may think of fitness as a physical thing, in truth it impacts every aspect of our lives, from bodily health to mental and emotional wellness.

When you exercise, your brain releases chemicals that reduce depression and encourage a relaxed, positive state of mind. Your self-worth and confidence also rise, because you know you're taking care of yourself. It feels good to do something as meaningful and important as taking care of your health.

In short, fitness makes you feel more energized, enthusiastic and able to take on the world. Why not commit to 30 minutes today? It could be just the boost you need.

January 27

"Women, with strength to carry the world yet the tenderness to comfort."

Strength and tenderness make a unique combination! But let's face it. We are tough yet tender, every day. We maintain strength in the face of adversity and help carry our loved ones through rough times. And, if they stumble or need support, we're there with soft, sensitive words and open, comforting arms.

Be proud of your ability to be both strong and gentle. Embrace these different sides of your personality and exercise them in equal measure. Show your strength and determination.

Be wise enough to step up to the mark yet let your gentleness shine through!

January 28

"Your skills, talents and expertise are everywhere."

At work, it's easy for your valuable skills and knowledge to shine. But, the truth is, your abilities and expertise reach beyond your work.

Your emotional, intellectual, social and organizational skills are just as valuable as your work-related skills. These are skills and talents developed along the rough road of life. Don't discount them. Cherish and nourish these skills; you'll gain a stronger sense of balance among all the demands of your day.

Remember, happiness and satisfaction surround you when your wisdom is treasured, whether it's work related or not.

January 29

"Life won't deliver what we expect."

There is no silver platter or silver spoon with your name on it. In other words, if you're sitting around waiting for the dues you expect from life, you may be waiting forever and end up with nothing but disappointment and regret.

Instead, be grateful for the fact that your life is what you make it. Relish and rejoice in the power you hold in your own two hands. You are the one that can go out and make things happen. So why not dare to seize new opportunities and enjoy the satisfaction they bring?

You alone hold the pen that will write your life story. Start a brilliant new chapter, today!

January 30

"Do you set goals then fail to achieve them?"

Too many failed attempts may lead to frustration. Eventually, you either stop setting goals or surrender to the failures that overcome you. Overtime, avoiding disappointment becomes easier than setting new goals, altogether. Your heart wonders, what's the use in trying?

Let your next goal be different. Before you start, break your ultimate goal into smaller goals. This way you're placing your expectations of success on your immediate goal, rather than the whole project.

By breaking down your goal in to bite-size pieces, the whole can be achieved much more easily. With each milestone, you feel energized and motivated to keep on going.
Instead of being stressed, frustrated and disappointed, you can now feel good, because you have a doable method to achieve your goals that works like magic!

January 31

"Infuse tranquility into your life and relationships."

Accepting responsibility for what you are feeling is hard, especially when what you are feeling is anger. If you leave angry feelings unresolved, they may turn into resentment, envy, jealousy, revenge and eventually hatred. These emotions also lie at the root of depression. And, who wants that?

Is there something that repeatedly makes your blood boil, that you end up screaming and yelling about, every time the subject comes up?

Ask yourself if you're overreacting or taking something too seriously. If you still feel your anger is justified, change your response. The relief that comes after screaming and yelling is short lived.

Look for more constructive ways to vent. For starters, try talking your way through your anger, instead of reacting with rage.

Be proactive, take charge, be calm and bask in the light of serenity.

February

February 1

"Appreciate the women under your skin."

The nurturing, caring, mother...the passionate, exciting vamp...the romantic dreamer...the playful child...the determined go-getter...the loyal friend - all these women and more are inside you.

Acknowledge and treasure each one!

Give each of your inner women time and opportunity to surface, for each has wonderful things to offer and makes you so lovable.

Make time for nurturing, passion and romance. Follow your goals and let nothing stop you. Find opportunities for friendship and fun. Respect all your inner womanly strengths and values.

Be proud of these things, for together they create one truly amazing woman. That woman is you!

February 2

"Inspire yourself! Dress up your space."

Most likely you have a place where you spend most of your day, either your desk at work or a nook at home. If it's dull, cluttered or messy, your mood tends to be the same.

Look around. It may just be time to make some changes. Any positive adjustment to your environment will affect the way you feel.

What can you do to spice up your space and make it more pleasing? For starters you could dress up your office or home with a colorful plant, some fragrant flowers or even a photograph of yourself in a special place.

Whatever you do, make sure it brings a smile, both on the outside and the inside.

February 3

"Courage is acting in spite of fear."

We all feel fear at some time or another. It cannot be denied. Fear is a natural emotion in the face of possible danger, whether it's the risk from actions that could threaten our lives, or from new experiences that could threaten our happiness.

A courageous woman knows that courage is not an absence of fear - it is acting in spite of fear. She acknowledges the fear she feels and is determined not to let it stand in her way. Become that woman!

Accept that risk is the price you pay for the chance for new opportunities and new beginnings. When you acknowledge your fear and push past it, you'll reach all your goals.

February 4

"Exhausted by perfectionism?"

Why is it that adults feel they must excel at everything they try? Why must we be competent or skillful to experience success and enjoyment? Is perfection that important?

Face facts! No one is born perfect at anything, so, striving for perfection can create frustration and disappointment. Perfectionism is a heavy weight to carry and something we would never require of a child.

Watch children that are learning a new game. They know that doing things imperfectly is part of the learning process, that trying new things leads to new insights, a new way of looking at things and new skills. Instead of being embarrassed by failure, they laugh, jump up and try again.

When we let go of perfection and allow ourselves to do things imperfectly, we come to see how perfect we are, just the way we are! It's a subtle difference but it's true. Our lives become more perfect when we let go of perfectionism.

February 5

"You deserve to be pampered."

To pamper yourself you don't have to take the whole day off, you can simply integrate small moments of pampering into your everyday life.

Sometimes you just need a break, to catch your breath and restore your natural rhythms.

Pampering is not a forbidden pleasure but a necessity. Think of it as something you need to do, for "You."

Go ahead. Indulge!

February 6

"There are hundreds of languages in the world but a smile speaks them all."

A smile not only crosses geographic boundaries, it also crosses the boundaries of culture, background, age and beliefs. What's more, it works the same magic in them all!

A warm smile can make a child feel better, as surely as it can cheer up an old man. It can soften hearts and firm up commitments. It can mend friendships and break tensions. It can reassure and give support. It can say 'I love you' and 'congratulations.' It can make deals. It can make friendships. It can make memories or even make your day.

But perhaps, most important of all, a smile can make the world a better place for the person who gives it - you!

February 7

"Age is something that doesn't matter – unless you're a bottle of wine."

You are only as old as you think you are. If you embrace new opportunities, seek new learning and stay motivated and lively at heart, you can still do anything. In fact, given the wisdom and experience you've amassed over the years, you can probably do more today than you've ever been able to do before!

Keep your body lively through healthy diet and exercise. Nurture and exercise your mind with new experiences, new information, new friends, interests and challenges. Stay in touch with the world and no matter what your age, the world will stay in touch with you!

February 8

"Do you love, respect and trust yourself?"

Can you answer this question with an undeniable, resounding YES? Self-esteem is all about love, respect and trust. It's based on the confidence and satisfaction you have in yourself. Self-respect is the voice inside that tells you how special you are, that you can become whatever you want, and says it with conviction.

Learning to love the real you unconditionally, just as a mother loves her children, can take time. But you can do it! You'll know when you have done it, because your self-esteem will soar and you will be more creative, friendly, loving and outgoing, as a result.

Start loving, respecting and trusting yourself right now and never stop. You're worth it!

February 9

"We are all a part of each other."

As human beings, we were created to be part of a larger community. Belonging to a community brings purpose to your life and feeds you with energy, life and joy. This community doesn't have to be made up of family - it can be a monthly book club, girls' nights out or card games with friends; anything that connects you with people who share your interests, values and vision.

Let yourself fully experience the feeling of synergy that comes from spending time with these people. Feel the sharing, the mutual commitment and enjoy the company of like minds and kindred spirits.

Appreciate how the sum of a community is far greater than its parts. It's an incredible feeling. Don't miss it!

February 10

"Take time out for fun!"

When you were a child, you didn't look for a purpose in everything you did. You didn't run across a field, sink your teeth into a juicy orange or jump high with a ball because it was good for you. You did it for the sheer, glorious fun of it!

Release your inner child. Take time to play in the park, laugh with friends, visit a fair, walk barefoot on a beach...just for fun. If it makes you feel happy, that's all the reason you need. And, have fun!

February 11

"Teachers are all around you."

We often make the mistake of thinking super-achievers are the only people who can teach us anything. We forget about the single mom next door, who can teach us perseverance; the old man walking slowly in front of us, who can teach us patience; the child playing in the mud, who can teach us that a little dirt isn't the end of the world.

You can also gain wisdom from others' mistakes, thoughts, ideas and actions. There are learning opportunities galore all around you, but you need to be open and willing to receive and act upon them.

Instead of jumping to conclusions that something isn't relevant to you or telling yourself that you already do something as well as you can, take a new approach.

Take a closer look at those around you and ask yourself, "What can I learn?"

February 12

"Touch hearts with your intangible gifts."

O ne of the most treasured gifts of women is the ability to give, without expecting something is return. Such unconditional gifts of the heart, like encouragement, hope, love, a kind word and appreciation, fall into this category.

The glow you get inside when you share these gifts is comparable to nothing else. Your soul becomes filled with a sense of calmness and the burdens of the world seem weightless.

For what we give returns to us, multiplied many times over. So, cast the bread of kindness on the waters of life. Enjoy sharing a moment of selfless affection with someone in need.

That warm glow will always reward you. It comes with the principle of selfless giving.

February 13

"Has your ship arrived?"

A re you waiting for your "ship to come in?" It could be a long wait. Why not put your swimsuit on and go out and meet it?

Nothing leads to more disappointment and bitterness than the belief that you're owed something in life. Why wait for fate to somehow deliver unknown future bounties and success? Start focusing on what you can do to make things happen, right now.

Be grateful for the fact that you're in charge of your own destiny – and no one else has this power. Celebrate each success you achieve and pause to enjoy each moment of good fortune.

When setbacks occur, shake them off and move on. Fill your life with positive energy, not by making plans for the future, but by living for today.

February 14

"The ones you love don't always know it."

We have hundreds of ways to express our feelings, through words and gestures both large and small. All too often, however, we keep our feelings to ourselves assuming that those we care for know how much they mean to us. The truth is, they often don't.

The next chance you get, tell that special someone how much joy they bring into your life. Let them know how special they are to you. Make sure you give a hug and get a hug.

This will deepen your appreciation for one another and brighten your relationship.

February 15

"It's time to change and open up to new possibilities."

Are you aware of the abundant possibilities your life holds for you?

Most likely you are and you truly want to take advantage of the possibilities, but something is holding you back. When opportunities arise, it's common for women to decide not to rock the boat and hold on to stability and security.

Stability and security are like prison. They keep you where you are. Decide right now that you will take intelligent and calculated risks that push you beyond your comfort zone into a realm where you have refused to go until now.

Open your arms to new experiences and dare to find out what is truly possible for you.

February 16

"Humor is a necessary ingredient in life."

Humor is not just about telling, listening and laughing at jokes, although they too have their time and place. It's about perceiving and chuckling at the absurdities of everyday life.

These absurdities can range from everyday hassles to real heartaches and even hard times. Within each experience, there's something to laugh about.

Next time you find yourself getting uptight, relax for minute and look for this lighter side. There is always humor embedded in life experiences. When you recognize it, it becomes so much easier to put life's difficult times in perspective.

February 17

"Complement your busy life with movement."

Day after day, you balance the demands of your professional and personal lives, like working, personal relationships and home life, just to name a few. With all these priorities, your body gets neglected and exercise becomes just another chore.

But exercise is just what you need to keep your sanity. After exercise, you feel better, sleep better and become more energetic. Not only is your body healthier, but your mind becomes healthier, too.

If you think that there is absolutely no time for exercise, then find small ways to sneak it into your day. Start by walking up the stairs rather than taking the elevator. Or, take your sneakers to work and use your lunch break to walk with a friend. Even brief breaks to the water-cooler count.

You deserve to take care of yourself. You need it, your body needs it and your mind needs it. So, make a move, today!

February 18

*"You cannot live long enough to make all the mistakes.
Learn from the mistakes of others."*

In every mistake, there is learning, but not every mistake has to be your own. Just as society uses history to learn from the mistakes of earlier generations, so can you. Save yourself some time and frustration and look to those around you and learn from their experiences.

For instance, instead of being defensive when an older person passes on advice listen and appreciate the learning they've gained over time. Tune into their mistakes more closely than their successes. Reflect on why things went wrong and tuck the learning away in your mind for your own future challenges.

By avoiding the mistakes made by others, you can create true success for yourself in a lot less time.

February 19

"Completion comes from within."

Most women have the bad habit of looking to relationships outside themselves for validation. We believe that the love others give us is more important than the love we give to ourselves.

This puts a tremendous burden on those around us. If you really think about it, we cannot honestly expect someone to fulfill this demand. When we do, we are doomed to disappointment.

Instead, recognize that eternal happiness and a true sense of value can only come from within. The bottom line is that there is nothing anybody can say or do to assure you of your value if you aren't sure of it yourself.

Start taking time to appreciate yourself, what you have achieved and how far you can go. Rely on the power that shines from within. It will never let you down!

February 20

"Adventures, especially into new territory, are scary."

A re you anxious about a new job, a new responsibility, a house move or some other life-changing event? Relax! New adventures make everyone nervous. When you reach beyond your comfort zone, away from what's familiar and comfortable, anxious feelings are inevitable.

At such times, remember, fear is connected with joy.

We need new experiences to keep our minds fresh. We need new opportunities to feed the creativity of our souls. We need new adventures for personal growth.

Recognize that, through these experiences, you discover new parts of yourself. You might just reveal strength, courage and resilience you didn't know you had, and how great is that?

So, reach past your fear and celebrate what your new adventures may bring!

February 21

"Free yourself from anxiety by chasing away the What-if's?"

W hat-if?" So many negative thoughts start with these two words. "What if I'm late for work?" "What if I don't lose weight?" "What if I don't go to my friends for dinner because I'm too tired?" What if...what if...what...if!

Each anxious thought leads to another anxious thought, and another - only to feed a negative spiral of worry. Before you know it, your heart races, it's hard to breathe and there's a knot in your stomach the size of a pot roast.

Catch yourself! Next time you fall in to the "what-if" trap, stop it in its tracks. Turn your thinking in a positive direction. It takes time and consistent practice, but the freedom from anxiety is well worth the effort.

February 22

"The best possible preparation for success is a strong and positive self-image."

Think back to when you were young and received encouragement from a parent, teacher or coach before an exam or big event. They told you that you could do it and without hesitation you believed them!

You felt more confident and better equipped to achieve the success they said could be yours. Well guess what? This will still work today. And even better, you have a coach with you, deep inside, every moment of the day – your inner coach! Now is the time to trust her and let her guide you, it's one of the best things you can do for your self-image.

Remind yourself of your achievements in life - the career goals you've met, friendships you've built, the home you've made or places you've visited. These all are amazing accomplishments and have happened because of the incredible skills and talents you possess. The more you remember these triumphs, the stronger your self-trust becomes and the more you will achieve.

February 23

"Assertiveness is a matter of self-respect."

When you trust your assertiveness, you have the ability to express yourself and the ability to communicate your feelings, wants and needs. You are less dependent on others and more in control of your own life.

When you assert yourself, you make your own choices. You make room for your confidence to explode. Practice confident assertion by saying, "Yes" to the things you want to do and "No" to the things you don't.

Don't be afraid or feel guilty for asserting yourself. You have nothing to lose. You will only become stronger and more self-sufficient and in turn your self-respect and self-worth will shine!

February 24

"You look fabulous!"

The way you dress makes a statement to others. And, it is also makes a statement to yourself. The way you look affects your attitudes and actions. So, take the time to look great!

When you look better, you feel in control and optimistic. When you are proud of your appearance, you naturally walk with your head high and express yourself with confidence.

Each day is an opportunity to improve yourself. Today, why not take pride in your personal appearance? Reveal your good taste and watch yourself go from invisible to invincible!

February 25

"Cultivate your sense of humor."

A sense of humor is recognized as one of the key attributes that build personal resiliency. It's instrumental in helping us cope with change and other challenges. It's not really surprising. We all know how much better we feel after a good laugh! It releases tension, puts things back in perspective, and generally helps us take a more positive attitude.

Seek ways to bring out your sense of humor. Rent comedies, read the comics, watch children at play, and spend time with friends who see the funny side of life.

Laughter is wonderfully contagious. Why not spread some yourself?

February 26

"Commitment is a way of life."

The ultimate commitment is the one you make to yourself. Today, make the commitment to yourself to take full responsibility for your life and to make the most of it.

Remember time waits for no one. The choices you make and the actions you take, today, determine your tomorrows.

Say farewell forever to excuses, indifference and regrets. Stand up, claim what you want and get ready to do what it takes to get it.

In other words, commit yourself and never settle for less than your ideal.

February 27

"Find the lessons within your failures."

It's unrealistic to expect to have success in meaningful things you do and not have failures along the way. It's the way of life.

Instead of fighting it or feeling ashamed or guilty, accept this with grace. Look for the lessons to be learned - lessons not to be repeated and lessons showing you how to do it right the next time.

Any failures that you experience can be transformed into something of worth. It all depends on how you look at it.

If you remain focused and determined, these lessons become stepping-stones to the success that you seek.

February 28

"Listen - and your intuition will lead you to great places."

Everyone is blessed with the inner wisdom of intuition. But, too often, our logical mind takes the command post and we neglect to listen.

Next time you have a decision to make, sit quietly, without any distractions. Reflect on what your intuition is trying to tell you.

If you have a sense of doubt but you can't quite put your finger on it, don't question the "Why." The answer will come. If something inside you says go for it, follow that hunch. Don't think about all the reasons why you shouldn't.

Trust your intuition! It won't let you down.

In due time, the reasons "Why" will become crystal clear. In the meantime, your intuition will act as a golden compass pointing you toward your dreams.

February 29

"Clean out your mental closet."

R emember when you last cleaned out your clothes closet? It was tough at first, but afterwards you felt great. You got rid of those impulse buys that never worked and retired those too-tight jeans that you knew you would never fit into again. Remember how you felt? No guilt or regret just wonderfully cleansed and organized.

A mental cleaning is even more effective. It's a great time to get rid of the bad and the ugly. Throw out all your old beliefs, memories, limitations, guilt, fears, doubts, and images that are no longer serving you. Make room in your mental closet for all the good things that life has to offer.

When you start afresh, with an open and positive mind, you'll instantly feel energized and uplifted because all the negativity is gone. Try it!

March

March 1

"Start each day balanced and peaceful."

In the morning, it's easy for our minds to kick into high gear, by pursuing a list of important tasks. Within a few minutes, we're frantically running around trying to get everything and everyone organized.

But, when we start our morning by filling our minds with high voltage activity, we usually spend the rest of the day feeling anxious and stressed.

Instead, take a break. Tomorrow morning, set aside a few moments to fill your mind and soul with calm. Before you jump out of bed, enjoy a few minutes of peaceful relaxation.

Reflect on the importance of harmony, serenity and balance in your life.

When you start each day this way you'll have more energy and tolerance for what lies ahead. And, you'll be able to handle the unexpected with ease.

March 2

"Today...delegate everything you possibly can to others."

As women, we often try to do everything. For some, it's wrapped up in self-esteem. Some believe that the more we do, the worthier we are of love and respect. For others, it's a matter of control. Whatever the reason, the result is that many women end up juggling an impossible number of balls!

Vow to change today. Entrust your children with responsibilities; let family or colleagues take over joint challenges. Trust your partner to organize social events for the crowd.

They'll appreciate the confidence you have in them - and you'll get a well-earned break!

March 3

"Open your arms to change,
but don't let go of your values."

As you race through life, facing daily challenges and trying to stay on top of change, it's not always easy to find time to reflect on the values you hold dear. But, in truth, moments of change are exactly the times when you most need to remember values!

Women with a solid value system are generally happier and find it easier to overcome challenges. Values like integrity, loyalty, faith, compassion, courage and a sense of community, all work together to give us inner direction and purpose.

Values build personal resiliency, which in turn helps you bounce back from adversity and embrace new opportunities. Take a moment today to reflect on your values - and then go out and put them into action!

March 4

"What is true beauty?"

The true beauty of a woman is not in the clothes she wears, the figure she has or the way she styles her hair. It is in the way she sees herself.

Was Mona Lisa really a beautiful woman? Did it matter? She clearly saw the beauty in herself and Leonardo da Vinci captured the smile that said it - and that made her beautiful to all.

All women have this capacity to be beautiful. Feel serene and peaceful about the woman you are and be proud of your strength, your gentleness, your caring and your passion. Love your capacity to love and take joy in your capacity to feel and give joy.

Know that you are a beautiful woman... and the whole world will see it, too.

March 5

"You're not alone in the journey of life."

There's not a woman in the world that hasn't had to struggle or overcome difficulties. We all face challenges and adversity. When the struggle seems too long or too hard, remember, you're not alone.

At this very moment, you may face money difficulties, health problems, career challenges, or conflicts with children, partners or family. It's all part of life! And, many other women face the same issues every day. When we recognize that obstacles are part of our journey, when we recall that women we admire also carry similar burdens, it is easier to keep on going.

Tap into the strength that comes from knowing others experience what you experience. Stay strong by recognizing that you are one of millions of women who do their best to handle challenges, every day.

Don't let difficulties stop you and never give up. Instead, think of them as milestones that, once passed, will bring you closer to your goals.

Remember, every woman struggles as she walks along the road of life. But, so many heroic women are on this same journey that no woman walks alone.

March 6

"Happy women embrace change."

If you accept change, you allow circumstances to just happen to you. On the other hand, when you embrace change, you take charge and gain ownership of new opportunities. When you're in the driver's seat, your life is both more fulfilling and peaceful.

Recognize change for the positive effects it can have on your life. It's the engine that propels you toward new and better things.

You need change. So, look for it, seize it and embrace it with enthusiasm. When you ride on the crest of change, you reach your destination sooner and feel better about the journey.

March 7

"Stop the world and take in the beauty around you."

Most of us are so involved with the tasks that must be accomplished by tomorrow, that we miss the beauty of today. Loveliness all around us gets taken for granted. We rarely look up from our daily tasks to appreciate the treasures of our environment.

Take a moment from your hectic schedule, and smell the flowers. Watch the graceful soaring of a kite or even marvel at the stars.

You'll be surprised by the freedom you feel and the peace that it brings to your soul.

March 8

"Dissipate fear of failure by rediscovering the child within."

Look at a young child working on a project - cutting with little plastic scissors, drawing with crayons, taping the loose ends, with never a thought of failure.

No matter what the outcome, a child always feels a sense of pride and accomplishment.

This same child is within you; the child that does not worry about failure or being judged for trying.

It's not very often that things turn out right on the first try. That's okay! Just accept that trial and error are part of the process and learn from your mistakes. Children persevere, try again and learn.

The secret that every child knows is that there is no such thing as failure. Now you know it, too!

March 9

"A strong self-image requires a strong support system."

While each of us is responsible for our own self-image, it's important to have support, encouragement and inspiration from those we value.

Nothing erodes your self-image more quickly than unhealthy or destructive relationships. Seek out those who only want the best for you. Spend time with friends who cheer you on to reach your potential.

Nurture friendships that are positive and uplifting. Look for friends that listen attentively, that believe in you and encourage you. Your self-image will grow stronger until you can reach any goal!

March 10

"Grow up and laugh at yourself!"

When you were young, the worst thing that could happen was the ridicule of others. Looking back, you can recall the embarrassment and humiliation of being laughed at. And, God forbid that you made fun of yourself. It didn't happen.

But, as we grow older, we gradually learn that laughing at ourselves is okay. This is an important lesson. A lesson that, all too often, we forget to live.

Next time something doesn't go your way or you do something you regret, no matter how upset you feel, say to yourself, "In time, I will laugh at this."

You don't always have to wait for time to pass. Decide to laugh about it right then and there. Laughing puts things in perspective and chases embarrassment away. So, laugh at yourself, today!

March 11

"The power of your imagination can make things happen."

Imagine this! You're faced with a giant obstacle and you turn it into a personal triumph. Everything turns out beautifully. How do you feel? The emotion that accompanies conquest is hard to beat! So, what made it happen?

Events tend to play out in reality the way they play out in our minds. The exact details of the situation may vary, but the end result will be just what you imagined.

Next time you find yourself in a situation where you really need to succeed, describe to yourself the details of the outcome you want. Don't cloud your thinking with what you don't want to happen. Focus solely on what you do want to happen.

Revisit the outcome in your mind as often as you can. Your imagination will guide you to success.

March 12

"A sense of purpose makes life meaningful."

Is your life synchronized with your dreams and actions? Do you use the power of each day to pursue the dreams that matter most? If not, why?

You have a specific, unique purpose and destiny in this world. It's up to you to pursue it.

When you feel a strong sense of purpose, it brings direction. Achievement, hopefulness, motivation, persistence and high self-esteem then come naturally.

Stay grounded and focused on your daily goals and intentions. Don't get distracted; don't let anything get in the way. Align your actions with these callings and you will achieve your life's purpose, with ease.

March 13

"A powerful woman doesn't have to prove she is powerful."

Women who feel the need to prove their power usually worry, secretly, that they hold no power at all.

Deep down, they're trying to prove something to themselves. And the more they continue down this path, the more they prove their doubts correct!

If you find yourself trying to prove your power to others, stop. Let your power make itself known, through your quiet, calm confidence and the respect that surrounds you.

Remember, true power doesn't need to shout to prove itself. It can whisper and still be heard.

March 14

"Think life is hard - and it's hard!"

When you dwell on your problems or what you don't have, you generate negative energy, and chances are your life won't change for the better. Why not focus on the possibilities?

When you make up your mind to do something, you'll find you can. Instead of thinking about barriers in life, reach out after opportunities. Instead of seeing a locked door, see a key. Instead of thinking about the rough mountain climb ahead, see yourself standing on the summit.

Today, resolve to let go of the struggles and embrace your potential. Your shift in attitude will shift your life from the shadows into the sunshine.

March 15

"Be sensitive to timing."

While timing isn't everything, it is often the most important factor in determining how you and your ideas will be received.

In personal relationships bringing up sensitive issues when the other person is tired, not feeling well or thinking about something stressful, is risky. When you do, the chances that you will cause irritation and end up feeling rejected are high.

It's natural to assume that the negative reactions of others are signals that they don't care. But, in reality, you would probably react in the same exact way, given the same situation.

Be sensitive to when you bring things up. Don't let your excitement and enthusiasm blind you to the concerns and pressures of your partner or friend. When you want your partner's support, make sure the time is right. When you do, it's more than likely your excitement will be shared.

March 16

"Share intimate feelings and you'll never be alone."

Your friends and family are your closest links to personal freedom.

Through your relationships with them, you learn to love, to share, to care and experience true joy. Through these intimate connections, you learn what relationships really mean.

In times of sadness relationships comfort us, and in times of happiness they help us celebrate.

When you open your heart to another and share your deepest feelings, you open the door to personal freedom.

March 17

"Take time to be grateful."

Taking the time every day to recognize what you're grateful for helps keep things in perspective. Gratitude carries you through the tough times, and gives you the strength to surpass the stress of challenges.

Reflect on your family, your friends, or the place where you live, and the satisfaction they bring you. Think about your good health and your mental or physical talents. Consider the pleasure you received from a phone call with a friend or a laugh you shared with your children.

Look back on small and large moments - the affection of a pet, your success in the garden or a deep and fulfilling partnership. These are all things that nourish gratitude. And, gratitude makes life worth living!

March 18

"You're at your best in a supportive environment."

A significant part of your environment is the people you spend time with. These people have a huge impact on you and your decisions. That is precisely why you need to be sure you surround yourself with those who support you and your ambitions.

Do your best to avoid people who belittle your enthusiasm, put you down or try to squash your dreams. Do your best to seek out those that support your goals and share your infectious energy.

Surround yourself with positive people. When you combine that with both positive energy and attitude, you can't help but soar.

March 19

"Passion is the secret to motivation."

Did anyone force you to buy those great shoes, hug your children, kiss your lover or eat every crumb of that forbidden cake? Of course not - you did these things without a second thought, because you're passionate about them.

When you focus your life around things you're passionate about, no one has to motivate you. Internal struggles subside and your life becomes easier and happier.

Why not pursue a hobby you've always craved? Take up a cause that really matters to you or apply for a job you've always wanted. Get creative.

Reflect on what you love to do - and most importantly start doing what you love. Today!

March 20

"Who's in control, you or your emotions?"

When you allow your emotions to enter into discussions over conflicting opinions or positions, you cloud the issues and detract from your argument.

Even if you have a valid point of view, it becomes cloaked in feelings, which reduce its connection to rational thought. You risk losing the other person's respect. When you're emotional you end up handing control to those who are in charge of their emotions.

Next time conflict arises, stay calm. Bite your tongue, silently count to ten, take a deep breath and state your position in an objective and unemotional manner.

Remember, there is a time and a place for showing your emotions. And, powerful people keep their feelings undercover until the time is right.

March 21

"Slow down and enjoy the things that really matter."

Is your Outbox being squeezed shut by all the "to-dos" in your Inbox? Do you feel like there is not enough time in the day to get everything done? If so, it's time to simplify your life.

When you do, you have more time for the things that are important to you, like reading, traveling, entertaining, exercising, visiting with friends, etc.

Look for ways to simplify your daily chores. It can be done through better organization, changing some old habits, simply saying, "No," or even asking for help.

Slowing down is something you need to do, for your physical, mental and emotional health. So, take it slow – and enjoy!

March 22

"Believe in yourself and set your standards high."

Next time you're tempted to settle for something less than ideal - a man, a job, a home, a friend's behavior... perhaps even a pair of shoes - stop!

You're a woman of many talents and inner strengths. Your gifts enhance life and nurture so many. You deserve and are worthy of far more than second best. So, why accept less?

Never settle! Be discerning. Be demanding. Instead of lowering your standards, wait for the quality you deserve. The wait will be worth it.

March 23

"Walking is moving meditation."

If your life is going in a hundred different directions and moving a million miles an hour, walking may make the burden easier to handle.

Walking allows you to focus on being fully present. It provides you with an opportunity to mull over something that may be on your mind. It gives you a chance to take in the beauty and bounty that surrounds you. Walking can be a time for self-discovery, a time to reconnect with wholeness and harmony.

Take 15-minutes today, and just walk. Let your mind rest. Savor the physical and emotional benefits you gain from moving your body.

This is rejuvenation at its best!

March 24

"When the going gets rough, you need self-worth."

When you're looking good on the outside, with a new outfit or haircut, your day goes more smoothly and you handle setbacks more easily. This feels good and helps us handle the daily grind. But, tackling challenges is much easier and more dramatic when you feel good about yourself on the inside!

A strong self-worth builds personal resilience, which helps you face challenges and bounce back from adversity. You grow stronger from the inside out, and feel the confidence to persevere and move forward with enthusiasm.

So when things go wrong, don't reach for your credit card. Instead, reach inside for that priceless deposit of self-worth!

March 25

"Harboring resentment wastes time and robs your energy."

Holding grudges against another takes a tremendous amount of energy and slowly erodes your happiness.

If you think about it, it's also a waste of time. You have so many better things to do with your life.

When you allow your negative emotions to affect your daily thoughts and actions, you become controlled by them.

Take a check of the resentment you hold against your loved ones, your co-workers or even your neighbor. Try to overcome your resentment by letting your considerate and loving nature dominate thoughts and actions.

You can choose how to live your life. Free yourself from resentment and you will regain all of your energy. Try it. You'll feel great when you do!

March 26

"Not a woman in the world knows it all."

Let's face it - it's hard to learn anything when you think you already know it all. None of us like to admit our ignorance, yet most of us will confess that we don't know everything.

Once you acknowledge ignorance, you empower yourself. You can now take responsibility to chart a course toward greater knowledge. It's a beautiful choice.

As strange as it sounds, we often expect ourselves to know before we have learned, which creates anxiety and tension. Why not join other women that have let it go and are not afraid or embarrassed to admit their ignorance? Once you do, you'll relax and be more open to learning.

March 27

"It takes goals and motivation to win the race."

Do you know what is important to you? If not, you may have set unreachable goals or may not have set goals at all. Without meaningful goals, life is much like a race with no finish line. There is never any reason to celebrate!

If on the other hand, you set and achieve meaningful goals, you have many reasons to rejoice. Remember, even small goals count. You get to enjoy many moments of satisfaction and celebration. Your self-esteem and confidence get a boost, because you have proven to yourself that you are capable.

Determine what is important to you and resolve to pursue your goals with passion and persistence. The race is about to begin - and you want to win it!

March 28

"Depend on your inner guide."

When others give you advice, they may be right and they may be wrong. They may share your values and priorities, or they may not.

Rely on your inner judgment and intuition instead, and you'll stay on the right track.

You know inside what's best for you. If you follow this code, you'll stick by your principles, values and beliefs.

What's more, even if things don't work out, you'll have the comfort of knowing you did what you thought was best for you. And, that's always the right thing to do!

March 29

"We all need a special hideaway."

A special hideaway is where you feel at total peace and completely safe. Your special place could be a meadow or a beach or the bedroom you grew up in.

Try to imagine your special hideaway, right now. Look around and notice the familiar shapes and colors. Listen to the sounds and smell the fragrances. Notice the temperature and how your body feels.

If your special place is a beach, listen to the waves crashing against the sand. Hear the hiss of the foam as the waves recede. See and hear the seagulls above you. Notice the salty sea breeze, the warmth of sun on your skin and the sand between your toes.

When you go to your special place involve all your senses – sight, sound, taste, smell and touch. You'll feel revived, renewed and invigorated from the journey to your special hideaway.

March 30

"Motivation comes from doing, not thinking."

The longer you sit and think about doing something, the harder it becomes to do it. If you think too much, excuses may paralyze you.

Today is your day to stop thinking and start doing!

When you start doing something, positive energy flows and you become more motivated. So don't think about how you're going to exercise. Put on your running shoes and run! Don't think about how you'll learn a new skill some day. Go out and book a course, right now!

Stop procrastinating. Start doing! You'll find a motivation that can change your life!

March 31

"Take charge of your destiny, think 'I, Incorporated!'"

When you think of yourself as a company and your boss as a client, you not only build your value to others, you increase your personal satisfaction and decrease frustrations.

Suddenly, you're not forced to work or meet high standards because of your boss's expectations. Instead, you give your best because you choose to give your client superior service. You develop your skills to become more marketable to future clients. And you keep an eye on the marketplace, ensuring you're equipped to move on if better opportunities strike.

Change your mind-set today and let the entrepreneur within you shine. When you work for yourself, not only are you in the driver's seat of your future, your value increases by leaps and bounds.

April

"Hate is an invisible chain."

When you don't let go of hate, you let the thing or person you hate maintain control over you. You allow the hatred to keep the channels of negative energy open, sucking out positive emotions and holding you back from true happiness.

Cut off the hate and move on! When you cleanse your mind and soul of grudges and negative thoughts, you make new room for positive emotions and joy. Take a moment today to consciously let go of all hatred. Savor the new energy that you'll feel bursting through to take its place!

"Organize your time."

Getting the most from every minute starts with better organization. This means you need to be in tune with your immediate priorities and willing to stick with them.

As you go through your day it's easy to get caught up in busy work and less important errands. Instead, draw the line. You need to stay focused on your priority tasks. If making a list helps, do it. If it means telling someone you don't have time, then don't be afraid to say it.

At the end of the day, you will have accomplished what is important to you. You won't feel rushed, worn-out or stressed. Instead you'll feel energized, productive and accomplished. Then, you can give yourself a mental pat on the back for a job well done!

April 3

"There are no detours around obstacles."

There isn't a meaningful goal that can be achieved, without facing obstacles and hurdles. It's an inevitable part of life's road to success. The more you come to grips with this, the faster you'll get where you want to go!

Instead of seeing difficulties as the end of your dreams, see them as part of the journey. View obstacles as challenges, which, once overcome, will bring you closer to your destination. Refuse to be stopped - keep focusing on where you want to go.

When the going gets tough, remind yourself that snags build wisdom, perseverance and strength. With this outlook your frustrations will transform to motivations and success will come your way more quickly.

April 4

"You're as great as your thoughts."

Imagine your ideal self – a person filled with health, happiness and prosperity. Imagine living the life of your dreams.

This life is not as distant or unreachable as it may seem. You are a reflection of your thoughts. If you think you can do great things, you will. If you think you can't, you won't.

For change to happen you need to enlarge your thoughts. You need to hold a vision of yourself that will carry you through adversity and give you the strength to climb mountains.

So, hold your ideal self in your thoughts. Stay true to it. You will become as great as what you hold in your mind.

April 5

"Woman-to-woman phone calls last at least ten minutes!"

Of course they do! As women, we all have so much in our lives to share and so much to comment on. We have so much to laugh about - and sometimes so much to sigh about. We have so much comfort and support to give, and so much advice to ask for.

We have curiosity that needs satisfying, and insights that call out for discussion. We have burdens that need to be lightened and excitement that needs to be shared.

How could any woman be expected to do all this in anything less than ten minutes? Take ten minutes to talk to one of your girl friends, today!

April 6

"Only women know the difference between off-white, cream and ivory."

Imagine how dull life would be if you only saw things in black and white. What if all the infinitely wonderful shades that we, as women, are able to appreciate turned to shades of gray?

Our greater sensitivity enables us to find magic within the ordinary. Maybe it's our sense of style and innate creativity. Or could it be we know there's much more pleasure in having three colorful sweaters, instead of just one white one?

Never under estimate your abilities, your creativity and your sensitivity. With all these talents no one can deny that you are an amazing human being!

April 7

"Do what you love – and excitement will follow."

When you follow what you love in life, challenges can be tough because the stakes are high. You set your whole heart on reaching your goal and you want, so badly, to succeed!

It's not always easy. But, doing what you love means that, each morning, you awaken with passion and excitement at your core.

It means you're finding hidden strengths you didn't know you possessed. And, you're equipped to get over obstacles and disappointments with grace.

Most of all, it means no regrets. No matter what, you're living an exciting life, doing what you were born to do.

April 8

"Focus on your future instead of on what you missed."

It's important to look back on past successes but it's even more important to use your vision to look ahead.

When we spend too much time looking back at past events, we get caught up in the "woulda, shoulda, coulda" mental talk. Learn from your past and then let it go.

Focus your imagination on your future. When you send these good thoughts out in front of you, they prepare and smooth the way. Use your imagination to reel in all the possibilities that lie ahead.

Picture your ultimate success and then get to work creating it. When you take the giant step and dare to believe, your dreams will come true.

April 9

"Your bankbook is not a measure of your abundance."

Some of the world's most miserable women have the most impressive bank balances. Despite their monetary net worth, they lack the riches of love and the gifts of joy that others gain from simple pleasures.

Never under estimate the value of all that you have.

Recognize the priceless worth of the love and respect you receive from family and friends - and zealously guard it.

Take note of the wealth of self-esteem you gain from the work you do or the talents you exercise - and preserve it carefully.

Whatever your bankbook may say, you are a woman of substance and abundance!

April 10

"Accept fear and forge ahead in spite of it."

When we deny the fear inside, we keep it lurking there. It remains in our minds, quietly holding us back from reaching new goals or fully experiencing new opportunities.

Accept your fear - there's nothing shameful in it. Next time you shy away from a situation, stop and say to yourself, "I'm scared, but I'm still going to do it!"

As you acknowledge your feelings and keep going forward in spite of them, your self-worth and self-confidence will rise. The adrenaline from fear will change to the excitement of anticipation. Suddenly, you'll realize the emotion you're feeling has turned into sheer enthusiasm!

"You're richer than 75% of this world."

Many of us have dreamed of winning the lottery or fantasized about how happy we would be if only we had great wealth.

Compared to the bulk of the world, you are already enormously wealthy. You have possessions that most people only dream of and access to opportunities that many women can hardly fathom. You have food in the fridge, clothes on your back and a roof over your head.

You have the wealth that others desire.

So, as you go through your daily tasks, treasure and appreciate everything you have. You can't help but feel blessed when you look at your life through a window of gratitude.

"Thoughts, beliefs, and self-talk."

Can you believe that as many as 90,000 thoughts a day pass through our brains! Most of those thoughts are the same ones, over and over. The trouble is, that if the majority of our thoughts are negative, repetition will make them seem like truth.

The good news is that since we have the ability to program ourselves to believe negative things about ourselves, we also have the ability to program ourselves to believe in positive things.

As you go through your day, focus on the chatter going on inside your head. If you don't like what you're hearing, then stop, and consciously choose a brighter thought. As you become aware of your thoughts, it will become easier to program yourself to think in positive ways that serve you better!

April 13

"Silence is sometimes the best answer."

From an early age, we've all been taught the importance of problem solving. Yet, sometimes, we can help people more by not trying to find solutions. In fact, on occasion, silent listening and empathy can be a priceless gift.

People who are grieving the loss of a loved one or a relationship, need time to mourn, not quick solutions. They need you to listen while they pour out their hearts; they want a silent hug, not instant answers.

A friend who is ranting and raving about her partner may just need to let off steam. An understanding smile and a hand on the shoulder may be the best support you can give.

Why not try a little silence today? You may find it says more than a thousand words!

April 14

"Allow yourself guilt-free time."

So many times we live our lives doing what others want us to do or what we think is expected of us. This may be practical at work, where you need to fulfill your job duties, but your personal life is different.

If you're always doing what others want, you end up neglecting your own interests, needs and desires. Over time, your spirit withers and you feel caught in an undertow of survival.

You're important and so is the time you need for yourself! Pull out your calendar and mark some time off, just for you. Do it, even if it's only 30-minutes every few days. Consider this time an investment in your emotional health and wellness. Enjoy it without guilt, no ifs, ands or buts. This is time to give back to yourself!

April 15

"Life flourishes when you let go of resentment."

Resentment is like a parasite. It feeds on you and leaves you weakened by its presence. Its only purpose is to take from you - and take it will.

Break free and shake resentment off! There's simply no room in your life for this negative energy. You have so much to do and so many places to go. If you let resentment get in the way you'll never reach your potential.

Start by focusing on what you do have, not on what is lacking. Stop fretting about what should have been and concentrate on what could be. Forgive, forget and move on.

Let go of resentment today and you'll be amazed by all the space it leaves in your life for better things.

April 16

"Are you avoiding conflict?"

Do you avoid speaking your mind because you don't want to rock the boat? Do you feel it's just easier to avoid conflict?

When you don't take initiative and express your own wants and needs, others make decisions for you - and chances are, they won't always make the decisions you want! If this goes on long enough, you will start to feel misunderstood or taken for granted. Anger and resentment will grow and you'll eventually erupt.

You are the only one who can decide to change this behavior!

Next time you're asked what you want, don't rush to say you don't care. Stop and ask yourself, "What do I want?" Then, share it with conviction.

April 17

"The sooner you focus on your visions,
the sooner they will thrive."

We all know women with big ideas that can't seem to make them materialize. Are you one of these women? Big ideas and grand visions are never enough. They must be accompanied by a sharp focus.

When you focus on your visions, you gain a sense of personal power, a feeling that you are taking control of your life. Both self-respect and self-esteem get a definite boost, as you learn to consciously stay focused on the positive results you seek.

Don't waste another day! Stay true to your visions and never lose focus. Before you know it you will be living and breathing your dreams.

April 18

"Assertiveness is one thing – manipulation another."

Many women believe that to be assertive you must be manipulative. If this holds true, then assertiveness actually becomes aggression.

Recognize that being assertive isn't about being controlling. It simply means expressing your wishes in an appropriate, effective way, while maintaining the respect for others.

Keep in mind that assertiveness requires communication, negotiation and compromise. When you treat others with respectful assertiveness, you gain their respect in return. Try it!

April 19

"Take Five."

There's nothing worse than being overloaded with tasks and having minimal control over your amount of work, especially when you're feeling the pressure of deadlines. The longer this goes on, the more frustrated and unhappy you start to feel.

It's not worth it! You need to take care of yourself. Take a break if you need it, and get back in touch with yourself.

Something as simple as a five-minute walk can do wonders. It gives you time to think clearly, relax and put things back in perspective.

Remember, that you can only do what you can do, and stressing out over the impossible wastes the precious energy you need for the rest of your life.

So, take five, and feel glad to be alive!

April 20

"Get Motivated, Get Active, Get Fit!"

Have you ever noticed how much easier it is to stick to a lifestyle change when you do it with a friend? A friend sticks by your side and brings motivation, accountability and cheers of enthusiasm.

When you get fit with a friend, you have someone who shares your victories. You can both celebrate and be proud of your accomplishments.

Stop waiting for that perfect day to make some changes and join forces with a friend. Make the commitment to one another that you will stick together through thick to thin.

Eating well, being active and feeling good about yourself are essential to feeling healthy, alert and alive. You already know this. So why not start now?

April 21

"Happy relationships are all about attitude."

How many times have you heard yourself say things like, "I will be happy when he tells me he loves me," "Once he commits to me I will be happy," "I will be happy once he..." and so on. You get the picture!

Too often, we attach our happiness to the choices of others. When we put demands like this on our relationships, we give our power away. This is self-defeating.

Happiness is what you make it and it's within your control. You don't need a relationship to define it. And, in the end, this is what really attracts and maintains healthier relationships.

So, remember, your attitude is your foundation. When you're content within yourself, fulfillment follows.

April 22

"What you think and say determines your personal power."

Do you frequently hear yourself saying things like, "I can't do that," "It's beyond me," or "I am not the person for this task?"

If you express negativity often enough, your mind will believe it as truth. It becomes a self-fulfilling prophecy and the longer it goes on the more you will be driven by false beliefs. You'll be left feeling powerless and out of control.

Stop this vicious cycle!

Take notice of your inner chatter and vow to transform the "can'ts" into "cans." Your internal voice must support you and give you reason to believe in yourself. It must foster respect and drive your potential. You are a capable woman, capable of endless possibilities.

Harness your negative thoughts today and make the transformation that destines you to greatness.

April 23

"Change makes the difference."

If you want your life to be something other than it is right now, your only true option is change. Change takes courage and isn't easy, especially if you're feeling safe and secure with the way things are.

The hardest part about change is instigating it. This feels risky, but once you take that first step, you set things in motion.

Today, is your day to take that first step and stop letting life push you around. Today is the day you take charge of the changes you need to make in your life.

Start by identifying small things that you would like to change, just tiny things - things that are holding you back. Make a promise to yourself. Then, stick to that promise and watch yourself change. As you tackle small changes, your confidence will grow. You'll find that bigger changes don't seem insurmountable. And, most important, that change is rewarding and fun, after all!

"When you journey within, you're never without."

Your internal wisdom is the part of you that knows what is true and best for you. Each one of us is born with this gift yet it often gets lost in a sea of external voices, opinions and judgments.

It's time to recapture this priceless gift!

Make a time and a place when all you have to do is concentrate on yourself - not the children, pets, your boss, your coworkers, your unfinished laundry or your list of errands.

Make this special place a quiet zone and sanctuary. Close your eyes and listen to your thoughts. Be at one with yourself and quietly tap into your internal wisdom.

If this is new to you, be patient. It may take time. But, as you listen carefully, you will gradually come to know that the greatest wisdom is inside your heart.

April 25

"The life you live is the life you choose."

Y ou alone have the responsibility to shape your life. Your
happiness, success and fulfillment are in your very own
hands. You have the right to do whatever you want with it. What
an incredible gift you hold. Once you take ownership of it, you
realize that nobody can deny you this, except you.

Everyone ultimately has one boss and that boss is you. What
you tell yourself to do and the choices you make, shape your life
and destiny. No matter what the situation, you always have a
choice; this is the beauty of being in charge of you.

You hold the power to make your life great. Don't waste
another day. Use it!

April 26

"Optimism is a key ingredient for a healthy lifestyle."

O ptimistic women have it good; they're less susceptible to
ill health and better able to fight off ailments if they strike.
Given that stress and unhappiness can have a negative impact
on your health, it stands to reason that happiness resulting from
an optimistic attitude stands you in good stead.

Instead of looking at the black clouds above, think about the
blue sky beyond them. Instead of seeing a mountain with an
impossible climb, imagine yourself already standing on the
summit. In the same way you exercise to build physical strength,
keep exercising optimism to strengthen it.

Today is your day to start the world over. So, make it a healthy
one!

April 27

"The best decisions are made with your head and your heart."

We all agree that we should carefully and rationally think through life changing decisions. It's just as important when making these decisions not to neglect your emotional feelings.

When you carefully consider your feelings before making a final commitment you can save yourself a lot of heartache and frustration. There is peace in knowing that the decisions you make are the right ones for you when they reflect a balanced mix of rational thought and emotion.

Next time you're faced with an important choice, combine the power of your head with your heart. You'll know you made the right decision.

April 28

"Desire is your inner fire."

When you want something badly enough, nothing can hold you back! Obstacles may trip you up, challenges may tax your abilities, but desire still fuels your progress. Circumstances will present themselves as roadblocks, but if you want it badly enough, you will triumph.

The power of desire is the tenacious driving force that forms the cornerstone of commitment. It becomes the fuel for your perseverance and persistence.

Tune in to the strength of your desires, today. Success is as near as the power of your desire to achieve it.

April 29

"True success."

S uccess is not in your environment. It is not controlled by luck, chance or the influence of others. Success is not in the greener pastures on the other side of the fence. Success lies right where you are - here and now!

You don't need greater abilities or greater opportunities. You already possess what you need for success to develop deep within you. So, don't look elsewhere. Instead, expect the seeds of success to grow from your heart.

Starting today, vow to focus, explore and take action on what you have and what you can do. When you do, success will surely follow.

April 30

"Diffuse your anger with forgiveness."

W e all get angry and upset at times, even at the people who are our nearest and dearest. Imagine what would happen if you stayed angry and shut them out of your life forever. Your world would never be the same.

Forgiveness diffuses anger. Forgiveness strengthens character. So, even though there are times when forgiveness feels like the last thing you want to do, do it anyway. Even if the pain is hard to forget, remember, forgiveness is your only option for wholeness.

Forgiveness holds tremendous healing power and liberates the soul. When you forgive, you let go of anger, resentment and blame.

Invite relief into your life today. Forgive your way to happiness and peace.

May

May 1

"Focus on the joy."

How many things in your daily life do you do just for the joy of it?

When you do something just for the "joy" of it you are not worried about what you get in return, nor do you do it because you "should" or "have-to." You do it because you want to.

As you infuse your life with this kind of joy, you internalize the message that you cherish, love and respect yourself. Your self-esteem, self-confidence and self-worth all get a boost because you're doing things that are important to YOU.

Do something today, just for the "joy" of it. When you experience joy, others around you feel it too!

May 2

"Search for agreement."

Whether you are just making small talk with someone or conducting an important meeting, it is the search for agreement that puts the relationship into gear. All such talk is a search for common ground. "Isn't the weather wonderful today?" is one way that we search in everyday conversation.

Agreement increases momentum, just as disagreement may slow you down. So, before you sit down to talk with a loved one, colleague or even your child, plan in advance what you and the other person will likely agree on and be sure to bring those things up first.

Build your foundation of agreement and go from there. It is what skilled negotiators do all the time and so should you. The result will be strong relationships and most importantly, receiving the results that you need.

May 3

"It's not where you start; it's how you finish."

When looking at the big picture, we all know that how we finish is more important than where we start. Many successful people started out in life with the odds against them, and came through winners. They didn't let their starting situation determine their final outcome. Think about it...this same philosophy can apply to everything we do.

When working towards goals, forget that you may have started out at a disadvantage, met hurdles or made mistakes along the way. Move past the past! Don't get discouraged. Don't blame your past!

Stop looking back and start looking forward. Then, you will move ahead in leaps and bounds.

May 4

"Problem solving comes easier with a fit mind."

You wouldn't expect your body to stay in shape without regular exercise, so you can't expect your mind to perform to the peak of its ability without use.

This doesn't mean you need to start spending hours in the library or lose yourself in academia. Simply sharpening your observational skills and paying attention to the world around you will do wonders for keeping your mind in tune.

As you continue to learn and grow you'll gain the determination and confidence you need to confront any problems that cross your path. And, more importantly, you'll have a strategy and a plan to make things better.

Remember, keep your mind fit and creative solutions will come more quickly and easily.

May 5

"Cherish those that are closest to you."

Often, the things we value most become so much a part of us we forget to appreciate them. We take things for granted and never give them a second thought.

Have you ever called an acquaintance to thank them for something they've done, and never thought of saying thanks to your dearest friend for everything she has done?

Today is your day to reflect on the things and people that have done things for you. Take joy in your love for your children, your partner, your friends and other family members. Then, find a way to let them know how much they mean to you.

You'll feel great when you do - and so will they!

May 6

"Laugh - it feels good and it's good for you!"

Have you laughed yet today?
For most of us laughter doesn't come very often, yet the magic it performs on our well-being can't be denied. It helps you enjoy friends and family. It diffuses stressful situations and it allows you the opportunity to keep things in perspective.

In times of adversity, humor helps you to cope and survive. It helps you recognize absurdities in situations and eases the tension.

Recognize what makes you laugh and put more of it in your life. Let your sense of humor see the fun in everyday experiences and open yourself to silly and outrageous thoughts.

Allow your laughter to flow. After all, laughter is the best medicine.

May 7

"Change is expensive."

No matter what you want in life, you must give up something to get it. It's a universal law and it works like this. The greater the value of what you want the greater sacrifice you will have to make.

The truth is, that it is hard and continuous dedication that brings lasting results. There are no short cuts, easy streets or detours.

Expect to pay a price if you want to make your life better. But, more importantly, also expect to pay a price for just leaving things as they are.

May 8

"Save your energy for changing the things you can control."

Many everyday events are unavoidable and beyond our power to control.

Things like taxes you can complain about, but that doesn't make them go away. Traffic jams happen, especially, it seems, when you're running late. Bad haircuts are a part of life and happen to all of us.

It's better to accept with grace, as part of the journey, the things you cannot control. When tempted to control the uncontrollable, remember, the only thing you know you can always control is your response.

For example, in a traffic jam you can choose to honk your horn and scream, or you can choose to turn on the radio, listen to music, and calmly wait for traffic to clear. When you stop stewing over uncontrollable situations, you keep the vital energy you need to maintain a healthier, happier and in-balance you.

May 9

"We see the world as we are."

Remember the last bad day you had? Chances are you ended up in a grumpy mood and feeling fed up. Even though the sun may have been shining or people all around you were happy and laughing - you were miserable, which meant the day was bad no matter how you looked at it.

Unfortunately, this same thinking can color life itself. If you're facing hardship, you may feel life holds no hope. If you're lonely, you may decide the world is an unfriendly place.

Resolve to change this thinking pattern, now!

If you're depressed, think of the excitement that life offers. If you feel stressed look for opportunities with optimism in your heart. If you're lonely, realize the world is full of friendly people - and go out and meet them.

May 10

"Stop running to answer every request."

Does a ringing telephone, a doorbell or the sudden demand of an impatient coworker make you immediately stop what you are doing? Do you feel your tasks take second place to the requests of others?

Every time you "drop everything," your stress level rises and your productivity sinks. So, make sure these interruptions are vital. Demands on your life are often not as important as you think. What's important is "you" and what you need to accomplish.

It's time to get your priorities in-check and make a conscious effort to separate what's "important" from what's merely "urgent." Ask yourself, "Is this really important or could it be done later?" Give your attention to the things that really count. You'll find harmony when you do.

May 11

"Acceptance fuels change."

S ome of us suffer from painful relationships, dead-end jobs, or "survival" mentalities. The truth is that we aren't going anywhere because denial or blame keeps us stuck in misery. This kind of life is awful.

Think about your own situation. Are you using denial to survive dissatisfying consequences? Accepting and taking responsibility for mistakes and choices is not easy. It takes courage. But you must accept responsibility if you want things to change.

When you accept the reality of your situation, you take the first essential step to a new and better life. This is reason for celebration!

May 12

"There are no limits when you trust yourself."

T hink about the most self confident people you know. What is it that makes them that way?

Self confident people don't second-guess their capacity to succeed, nor do they wait for others to encourage them. They trust their own abilities to do what needs to be done.

Stop waiting for others to tell you what you can do. Start putting your faith in your own strengths and talents. Instead of questioning whether you can reach your goals, move forward with conviction and confidence.

You have incredible gifts. If you allow yourself to follow them, you'll achieve great things. Go ahead. Follow your abilities. They will lead you upward on a path that is has no limits!

May 13

"The secret glue that keeps relationships alive."

No matter how hot and steamy a relationship is at first, when passion fades there must be something more long lasting to take its place.

Most of us fall in lust before we fall in love. It's a wonderfully exciting time, when you need nothing more than passion to keep you glued together. Unfortunately, the reality is that lust alone doesn't make for long-lasting bonds. Such shallow desire disintegrates far too fast and easily.

The secret glue that keeps relationships strong, forever, is made of more powerful stuff. It's made of mutual respect, interests in common, of shared values and genuine friendship. And, it takes time to discover and nurture these important parts of a strong relationship.

So, rein in those passions long enough to determine whether your desire is more than skin deep. Remember, the secret glue that makes relationships last forever keeps your passion – long after the lust has gone!

May 14

"Choosing not to decide weakens your power."

Making a decision is one thing. Putting off making a decision until the moment has passed is something else. A decision made after thought or reflection has value. But, choosing not to decide is one more way to give your power away.

It's time you played an active part in life. So, take responsibility for future consequences. When you do this, you're empowered by the control you give yourself.

Remember, failing to make a decision drains your power away. It fuels fear and weakens your resolve. When you walk away from a decision simply because it seems too hard, you give up control. You become a passive onlooker instead of an active participant in life.

Have the confidence to make decisions. You'll come out stronger - whatever you decide!

May 15

"Is it better to give than receive?"

We have heard this cliché a million times. As a woman, you probably spend most of your day loving and nurturing those around you. Day in and day out you're probably giving all you have and taking good care of those that rely on you.

The trouble begins when you don't receive love and nurturing in return from the ones who receive your care. As time passes, it's only natural for you to feel resentful.

Does this mean you should stop giving because you are not receiving? Of course not! Instead, you need to make it known that you need the same love and compassion that you give to others, every day.

You too, need to be taken care of. Why? It's only when you receive this love that all your giving becomes effortless.

May 16

"Empower yourself by organizing clutter!"

Old medicines, stacks of books, clothes you never wear, Christmas cards from last year, piles of papers, towers of magazines and drawers full of who knows what. It's called clutter, and the more it collects the less you want to deal with it.

Clutter can overwhelm you and drain your energy.

Eliminating clutter is healthy. No longer do you pour energy into looking through papers for that one lost item. No more do you ignore anxiety about piles that disguise forgotten responsibilities. No hours of frustration are added to your preparation for the day, as you pull wrinkled clothes from your closet because they're wedged too tightly.

Suddenly, you're in control! You know where to find things and you're proud of your space.

Start clearing out your clutter today. Start small, by clearing out one drawer, one cabinet, or one shelf. You won't feel overwhelmed and the results will give you the motivation to tackle the next pile.

Organization is a gift that you deserve. Give it to yourself and get your power back!

May 17

"Smother your passions and you'll forget what you love."

Many of us have put aside our passions to focus on practical goals. That's okay, but be sure you're only putting them to the side temporarily, not smothering them.

You need to stay in touch with your passions, even if it's only long enough to remind yourself that you still have them. Take a one-day seminar, a weekly art class, attend a monthly reading club or go online and "chat" with folks that have similar interests, when you can. This will keep your passion flowing, without taking a large chunk of time from your schedule.

If you don't have time during the week, indulge your passions on weekends, vacations or holidays. Make it a goal to keep in touch with your passions. When you do, you will know how valuable you are and you will live in Technicolor, instead of black-and-white.

May 18

"Give the 650+ muscles in your body some attention."

We were given all these muscles for a reason - to use them! Without exercise, they become weakened and you become physically less than you could be.

Get out there! If you don't want to join a gym, that's fine - develop your own exercise regime. Jog in the park, play volleyball or tennis - swim, cycle, skip, ski or dance. Just get those muscles moving! You'll not only be fitter and more toned, you'll feel much better, as well.

And remember, those 650+ muscles include your "smile" muscles. They need exercise, too!

May 19

"Before you believe in yourself, you have to believe yourself."

No matter how often you mentally tell yourself that you're talented and worthy of respect, it won't get you anywhere if you don't believe what you're telling yourself.

The key to creating this belief is to provide yourself with rational support.

To build your rationale, list your achievements in life, right back to when you were a child. Write down the successes you have had no matter how insignificant they may seem. Take note of the generosity and love you've given to others. Think about how you've helped to enhance life, whether through your garden, motherhood or special talents and friendships.

Now you can tell yourself you're special and believe it, because your list is proof!

May 20

"Satisfaction comes from giving your wisdom away."

Each one of us can make a difference by passing on what we know.

You have something worthwhile to share, regardless of where you are in your life. You've built a history and you've learned lessons along the way.

It may be as simple as chatting with other women in the same situation and exchanging ideas. It may be giving talks and volunteering in professional organizations.

Never believe that you don't have something to give. You do! Serve as a role model inspiring and encouraging other women.

Pass on your confidence, moral support and hope to others. Immense satisfaction is what you'll get back.

May 21

"Clear your mind, dail, and appreciate the moment."

The more your life is packed with deadlines and stress, the more you'll benefit from taking time out to just 'be' in the moment.

Clear your mind of everything that's gone by and everything that's to come.

Focus on the blue sky above or the clouds racing by. Feel the warmth of the sun on your face or the cool of the raindrops on your hand. Look at the grass, the trees or the people walking by. Breathe in the scent of flowers.

For a moment, just 'be.' It will ground you and help you put everything else back into perspective.

May 22

"Laughter is the best medicine!"

Did you know that the average child laughs 400 times a day, while the average woman laughs only 15 times per day? If laughter seems like a distance memory, then it's time the child inside came out to play.

In reality, you have so much more to enjoy than the child you used to be - and so many more reasons to laugh. You have that vast library of memories to be brought out and explored - years of joy, adventure and smiles. There are mistakes filed away - all good reason for laughter. There's the accumulation of friendship - full of hugs, love and good times. There's that treasure chest of experience to be dipped into – and so much more meant to bring a chuckle!

And finally, never to be overlooked, there's that secret inner deposit of excitement, wonder, enthusiasm and confidence in all the good times yet to come!

May 23

"Don't let the unexpected control your attitude."

You wake up in the morning feeling great about your day. Then, you get in your car and it won't start, or you spill coffee on your new skirt just before a meeting, or the babysitter calls to say she'll be late.

And, that's just the tip of the iceberg. One after another, unexpected things happen until you want to scream!

Wait a minute; force yourself to relax and recognize the unexpected for what it is – one of life's surprises. Take a deep breath and rationally consider your options. Choose the most appropriate way to deal with the situation, and then move on.

When you slow down and take this calm approach, you're empowering yourself with control. And, soon, your attitude will brighten back to the eagerness and energy with which you originally greeted the dawn.

May 24

"Never please to appease."

Do you go to great lengths to please others or cover up your feelings, because you fear abandonment or rejection? If so, why?

The truth is, you run less risk of rejection if you offer others your true and unembellished self.

When you're up front with your real opinions, feelings and interests, you stand on solid ground. Being genuine offers others the real you, right from the get-go and they can choose to take it or leave it. Just as you can choose to take or leave them!

When you know others are responding to the real you, you no longer have to worry about letting down your guard or being rejected later. This is a position of great strength.

Try living as the real you! When you do, others are naturally attracted to who you really are!

May 25

"New experiences are opportunities to learn."

Each new experience opens doors to new possibilities. Yes, just the thought of stepping out of your comfort zone can be scary. But, it can also be extremely rewarding. Just think, waiting for you are untapped skills, fresh knowledge, new relationships and so much more.

If you face setbacks, as we all do occasionally, avoid thinking of them as failures. Instead, embrace the opportunity for growth and learning and keep forging ahead.

As you tread new paths and reach new horizons, your self-confidence will skyrocket. You'll no longer dread new experiences, but look forward to them with enthusiasm.

Come on! Throw your fear of failure out the window. Jump in feet first and reap the personal rewards of learning something new!

May 26

"Awareness is the power you need to take control."

Throughout each day you're constantly talking to yourself. It's completely normal. We all do it. In fact we do it so much that our subconscious mind accepts what we say as truth. This acceptance forms the beliefs that we have of ourselves, and how we perceive that others see us.

If your self-talk is negative, your beliefs about yourself will be also. On the flip side, if your self-talk is positive and self-empowering, so is the image and the beliefs you have of yourself.

Take time today and tune in to how you're speaking to yourself. Identify precisely what beliefs you're forming based on your self-talk and bring them to your conscious mind. Question them, scrutinize them, and become familiar with what are they telling you.

The awareness gained by doing this is the first major step toward an empowerment that will affect everything in your life!

May 27

"It's always uncomfortable to grow."

Many of the things that are required to build and maintain healthy self-esteem can be uncomfortable, but the truth is they are essential. The good news is, with practice, uneasiness subsides and they become part of who you are.

Saying "No," and asserting yourself, asking for what you want, expressing your true feelings, saying positive things about yourself, letting someone love and nurture you...these may all be things that are uncomfortable. But, only at first.

One sure way to conquer discomfort is to simply do what is uncomfortable. Step away from complacency and dare to grow and develop yourself today. Start by choosing something that you have been putting off. Then, just do it!

May 28

"Every woman sees the world in a different way."

Every woman sees her world with a different vision. In other words, someone else may assign a completely different meaning than you to the same thing. This is a blessing! Why? Because it means you have the ability to create whatever kind of world you want, just by assigning meaning to things in your life in whatever way you choose.

Imagine a picture of an old barn nestled in sweeping green grass, and white capped mountains in the back. What do you focus on this picture? The old barn falling apart that should be torn down, or the beautiful sweeping meadow with a snowy mountaintop in the background?

You assign meanings to all the people and things in your life. Ultimately, this is the breeding ground for your attitude. If you don't like what you see, change your vision. It's easy when you think and choose. Try it!

May 29

"Think big and bold; and hold on for the ride."

A ll dreams and aspirations start with a thought.
Thoughts may come to life gradually but those small thoughts are the beginning of something great. With time, your thoughts turn in to dreams and those dreams turn in to visions. Visions become the blue print for your life's aspirations and goals.

Your greatest achievements will always take place in the framework of your vision. So, it's essential to think big, dream big, and visualize big.

If you expand your thinking and your thoughts, your dreams and visions will grow to great proportions. And, when they do – hold on. You can achieve anything you put your mind to!

May 30

"What do you think counts?"

I f you're not sure, then it's time to rediscover what you feel is important. In other words, what fuels your passion?

To rediscover this passion, start by simplifying your life. Quit doing things merely out of habit. Turn off the TV for a month or turn off the radio while commuting to work. See where your mind takes you.

When you find yourself saying, "I love that," or, "This is fun," take note. That inner voice is leading you toward your passion.

Become comfortable with the idea of doing what you like. As you discover what you enjoy doing, you'll find answers to what counts for you.

And, that's what being passionate is all about!

May 31

"Be aware of road blocks."

When it comes to making changes in your life there are some things that can derail your progress and sabotage your efforts. The good news is, if you're aware of them, you're much more likely to overcome them.

Be concious of your "old thinking." Things like temptations, excuses and negative thinking. When you catch yourself in any of these traps, just stop what you're doing. Remember what your goal is and think about the progress you've already made.

Naysayers also work against your efforts to change. If you have pessimistic people around you that say you can't possibly lose weight, start a business, or improve your relationships, combat this by surrounding yourself with supportive people. Don't be afraid to assert yourself in these situations.

Sometimes, we have disagreements and go right back into our old patterns. Again, stick to your guns. Removing yourself from the situation can help you bring your determination back into perspective.

Roadblocks become merely bumps in the road when you are aware and prepared.

June

June 1

"Every woman holds the power to do great things."

Yes, it's true! No "if-ands-or-buts." Once you believe this, you set yourself free to achieve the meaningful things you want to do in your life.

If you are looking outside yourself for the key to success then stop! Success is already inside you and always has been. Right now recognize it and own it. Don't be afraid to step up and be yourself.

You deserve greatness!

June 2

"Friends and family build and nourish your success."

From your first breath, mind, body and soul were nourished by the family and friends that touched you.

Imagine what it would be like to reach your ultimate goal and have no one there to share your triumph and success. The thrill of such celebration means so much more when it's shared with those that are most important to you.

As you march through the peaks and valleys of life, allow friends and family to share in your journey. The sense of accomplishment and satisfaction you receive will be so much greater when you do.

June 3

"We only wish for others what we are willing to receive ourselves."

Women that are happy with their lives are much more likely to support and encourage your happiness. Women who have goals of their own are more likely to support you in pursuit of your goals. Women who express their creativity are more inclined to help you discover your own talent.

Armed with this knowledge, you can choose to associate with those that have your best interest at heart.

Look carefully at the lives of the women in your circle of friends. Do you "hang out" with those who choose scarcity or abundance? Perhaps, it's time to let go of friends who are unwilling to recognize happiness, to value goals, or nurture talent; and time to welcome healthier friends into your inner circle.

But, before you view your friends with a critical eye, take a long look at yourself. Are you happy, goal oriented, and in pursuit of your talents? If not, take steps to include these virtues in your life. You'll be amazed at how old friends may change and how new friends may suddenly appear.

June 4

"Life's only limitations are the ones you accept."

If you say you can't, you won't. If you say you can, you will. It's really that simple.

The secret is to stop looking at limitations as roadblocks. Instead, see all the opportunities life offers. Embrace them with the belief that you deserve them just as much as anybody. The truth is, you do.

Never be afraid to jump into new experiences. The potential rewards they offer you are unlimited; you just need to be willing to let them into your life.

Remember that a closed door is merely a door that hasn't been opened – break down the barriers and don't be afraid to barge right through with confidence. You can do it!

June 5

"Before you decide, review your values."

We all have wants, needs and desires. These feelings indicate what we value most. But, sometimes, wants, needs and desires come into conflict, and we must decide where to invest our time and attention.

No one can do everything at once. So, when a conflict arises, take the time to think about your long-term values before your make a decision about where to focus your energy.

Remember, when you focus on one thing, you often must let go of another (at least for the time being). Ultimately, you must go with the decision that supports your highest values, and will make you happiest, both now and in the future.

But, don't delay. Fulfillment and joy await you, after a decision is made.

June 6

"Fulfillment is the fruit of work that is more than a job."

Passion, a positive attitude, and a sense of adventure, excitement and fun, all make your work more than just a job.

There is no mystery in the fact that the rewards of work are greater when you're engaged in what you do.

Are you engaged in your work or is it just a job? If you dread your days in the office and feel like a robot going through the motions, then honestly ask yourself if this is how you want to spend your life.

Women who love what they do, take immense pleasure in their work experience. Achievements come naturally, and they feel refreshed and exhilarated at the end of the day.

Remember, you were born to do work that you love. So, do it. And feel the joy!

June 7

"To choose or not to choose..."

The older we get, the more we realize that the choice to be happy or unhappy is our own. Sure, there will be times where things don't go our way. We'll feel unhappiness, sorrow, even depression. But, our agency determines how we cope with these challenges.

This doesn't mean that we should feel guilty about being sad or depressed. Everyone experiences "down" days. Melancholy moments can bring great wisdom if we think them through.

But, the truth is that you always have a choice. You can choose to stay stuck in unhappiness and resentment, or, choose to let go and feel fulfillment lighten your load.

If you're unhappy, unsatisfied or merely ambiguous, make today the day you put it all behind you. Choose to feel the joy in your life again.

You always have a choice. Why not make it great?

June 8

"Personal growth is just a hug away."

We have all heard that you need four hugs a day for survival, eight hugs a day for maintenance, and twelve for growth.

The touch of a hug has a healing effect on your body. Your immune system stays strong and you feel loved and special. Hugs have a way of nurturing the little child within you and helping you feel cherished by family and friends.

If you're not getting your twelve hugs a day, reach out and ask for the hugs you need. A simple, "Can I have a hug?" goes a long way toward getting those twelve hugs you need for growth.

June 9

"Spend time alone, everyday."

To be fully grounded, you need to be in touch with yourself. You need to hear and listen to your inner wisdom and nurture your inner strengths and dreams - none of which is possible when you're actively focusing on the outer world.

Every day, find a place where you can be alone for a while. Shut off outside channels and be at one with yourself.

Count back from ten, letting the outside world stresses and thoughts leave, as you exhale with each count. Breathe in deeply and let the oxygen replenish your cells and your spirit. Feel the deep relaxation and contentment available at that moment in time.

When you give yourself this time alone, you'll discover a new level of energy you didn't' know you had. You'll also find the strength to manage challenges and enjoy the rest of each day.

June 10

"Go for it!"

There is no perfect time for anything, so what are you waiting for?

The truth is that now is as good a time as any to put your dreams into motion. Let's make today the day to begin your journey to greater levels of fulfillment and productivity. No more waiting for things to be "just right."

No matter what you have been putting off, make a commitment to yourself that today is the day to get moving. There will always be challenges and obstacles. So what! If you take things in stride and roll with the punches, you can overcome anything!

Remember that with each step you take, you'll grow stronger, more and more skilled, and more and more confident. Break free and go for it!

June 11

"Challenge yourself and take a risk."

One of the biggest roadblocks women face when learning new things is the fear of doing it wrong. We worry what others will think and fear being judged by our peers.

Unfortunately, this often encourages us to play it safe or not even try. So, many opportunities come and go, because we're afraid to look foolish.

If you want to grow as a woman, it's time to stop worrying. Growth requires you to let down your guard and stop being self-conscious.

The reality is that others don't pay as much attention as you may think. Even if they do, are they going to remember three weeks from now? Probably not.

Resolve to take a risk, to put negative comments out of your head, and most importantly, to forget about doing it wrong. If you let yourself, you will succeed - and inspire others to follow in your footsteps.

June 12

"Take time to think before you act."

When you find yourself getting angry or resentful toward your partner, it's natural to start blaming. First, you yell; then the argument escalates into damaging accusations.

Be aware that when you do this, it only perpetuates more hurt and anger. To avoid painful words, stop and think about how you feel and why. This will dissolve the negative energy, right away, and help you move to a place where you can focus on what is most important.

After you're clear about how you feel, focus on your needs. Ask yourself what you need to feel better about the situation. It may be as simple as a phone call, if your partner is running late, or a pocket organizer that helps your partner recall important dates.

Next time anger strikes, take a moment to focus on your feelings and needs. Share them in a non-threatening way, to replace hurt and anger with happiness.

June 13

"Decisions shape your destiny."

All the decisions you have made throughout your life have brought you to where you are today. That's powerful, when you think about it. In other words you manage your life by the decisions you make.

If you let others make decisions for you, then you're giving them the key to your destiny. That key is yours! You were born with it. It is your way to take charge and take control.

You're responsible for your life and you need to be in the driver's seat, especially when it comes to the decisions that affect your future. So, look to yourself first. Look to others for guidance, but ultimately there is no one better than you to decide what's best for your life journey.

June 14

"Stop feeling guilty about angry emotions."

We're often told that anger is an undesirable emotion. But, you know what? Sometimes it's justified.

If someone has crossed the line, you're entitled to feeling angry. It's perfectly normal and healthy. There is no reason to feel guilty about your anger.

Next time you feel anger, acknowledge it without self-recrimination. Give yourself permission to feel the rage. Because, when you do, you can work through it, release it and feel joy again.

June 15

"You deserve to feel like Number One!"

It's time to clean house and surrender any destructive thoughts in your head. No more will you allow negative people to scramble your brain. No more will you dwell on painful uncomfortable times.

Let go means - let go!

Make it a priority to keep investing in yourself and your well being. Make room in your life for happiness, success, healing and fulfilling relationships.

Before you know it, you will start feeling entitled to abundance. And, that is as it should be, because you are Number One!

June 16

"Peace of mind comes with daily discipline."

Cultivating peace requires discipline. Many women pray, some exercise and some meditate to achieve this goal. Whatever they do, each of these women has found sanctuary in their silence.

With silence like this you're able to relax your mind and body. You simply let go of the tightness in your body and the chatter in your head.

Why not try it? Start by focusing on a discipline. Once you feel the quietness surround you, let your mind and body relax.

Quiet time spent like this each and every day will do amazing things for your heart, your spirit, and your peace of mind.

June 17

"There will be times when all seems lost."

At one time or another it's likely you will feel that your life has hit a brick wall. You may feel there are no solutions to your problems and your life will never change for the better. This time may even be now.

During such times, you must look back and remember the past obstacles you faced and conquered. Remind yourself of how you confronted and overcame them. Those challenges seemed as difficult as the ones you may be facing now.

Use your memories to reassure yourself that things will change, that you will get through these hopeless feelings.

You did it before and you'll do it, again! Success is just around the corner.

June 18

"The true beauty of a woman is reflected in her soul."

You don't need a perfect figure, a huge and expensive wardrobe, or a brilliant hairdresser to make you a beautiful woman. Beauty is waiting there inside your soul, ready to be brought out.

Your joy in life and passionate pursuits make you sparkle and radiate excitement and energy. Your sexy confidence and enthusiasm light up your face and bring a swing to your walk. Your serenity, generosity and sensitivity are mirrored in your eyes and in your beautiful smile.

You are a beautiful woman - know it, believe it and live it!

June 19

"You cannot change anyone but yourself."

When people don't live up to your expectations, it's not unusual to feel responsible for changing their behavior, especially if they are close to you. You may try and try - but when you don't succeed, you end up feeling depressed and like a failure.

Changing another person can be a frustrating, impossible goal. Realize that people only change when they want to. Changing someone else is not your job!

When you put yourself in the position of controlling the uncontrollable you place a heavy burden on yourself. Not only do you feel weighted down, but you use up tremendous amounts of energy in this pursuit.

Instead, channel your focus toward things that you can control, such as yourself. It's a much more peaceful and productive way to live.

June 20

"Commitment is a decision."

Commitment is not just a simple act of wishing for something. Commitment is a decision to do whatever it takes.

You may wish to be in awesome shape. But, you won't succeed until you decide to put down the chocolates, get off the couch, and start exercising regularly!

Yes, this is hard to hear, but that's what commitment is all about – deciding to put in the sweat and effort and sacrifice, to achieve the goals you hold dear.

The sweat and effort may come from your head, as in commitment to your workplace or achieving your goals. It may come from your heart, as in commitment to a relationship or your children.

But, wherever it comes from, it requires a decision not only to start, but persevere. Remember, the rewards you seek are priceless and worth every moment of dedicated effort.

June 21

"Concentrate on what you want."

When you think about what you don't want to happen, it happens! Concentrating on what you fear and obsessing about negative outcomes has a way of manifesting disastrous images in your head. These images are very powerful and often turn into reality.

Instead, create pictures in your mind of what you want. Imagine the best possible outcome. Take a minute or two to do this every day.

When you focus your energy toward things you really want, rather than toward what you don't want, the universe will respond and deliver. Try it. It's an amazing phenomenon that nurtures your desires!

June 22

"Compromise and collaboration bring harmony."

When harmony is in your life and relationships, peace and serenity are at your fingertips. All your senses are alive. Your visions are clearer, and you can see more, feel more, and hear more.

But, harmony has one enemy - conflict.

When conflict arises and threatens to displace harmony, the best thing to do is face it head on. Don't ignore it. When you do, you allow it to fester.

Instead, recognize that those with differing views are not out to get you, but merely approaching things from a different point of view. Seek to find points of agreement and work together to build compromise.

As you focus on compromise and collaboration, harmony will be restored.

June 23

"Cultivate your talents."

Talent does not mean you have to be an artist who paints masterpieces or a gymnast who does flips. Talent resides within you, right now, in many different ways.

Caring for others is a talent, teaching is a talent, making people feel welcome is a talent, solving problems is a talent, and parenting is a talent.

Never underestimate your talents and try not to compare or wish for the talents of others. Focus on and accept the talents you have, and you will find great fulfillment in life.

June 24

"Have the courage to dream."

As a woman becomes a wife and then a mother, there are many things that she compromises - her dreams are just one of these. When there are diapers to be changed and homework to be supervised, where's the time to spend those few precious moments doing your own thing?

Many times we become so obsessed with what we ought to do, we forget about what we want to do. In the end, we even lose the courage to dream.

Take a good long look at yourself. Has the 'song' gone out of your heart? Do you feel like just getting away from it all?

If yes, it's time for action. Immediately!

Allow yourself some time for pure, undiluted pleasure. Let go of all the things that pull you back. Imagine yourself to be a gull in the salty breeze above the peaceful sea. Meditate, read, write, sing or paint - do your own thing.

In the new life you are creating, this will be the first step toward freedom and joy.

June 25

"Confidence is power."

Confidence is a strong powerful force within that gives you the ability to conquer life's obstacles. The power of confidence comes from your internal power plant and it's up to you to keep the fire going in times of doubt.

There is a saying, "Fake it till you make it." In other words pretend to be what you want to be until you arrive. If you feel like you have tried everything, try this. It just may be the missing piece to the puzzle.

Use this idea as an inspiration to stand up and tackle anything that you're unsure about. Fake if you have to. Just remember, it won't take long for the powerful force of your confidence to pave the way.

June 26

"Money isn't everything."

It's easy to fall into the trap of thinking that your life would be better, easier or happier if you had more money.

Wanting more money isn't something to be ashamed of. Money can give you the freedom and confidence to pursue your dreams. The trouble starts when you make money, success or prestige your only focus in life.

Your pursuit of money needs to be balanced with the other important areas in your life; things like family and helping in the community.

When you allow this balance into your existence you're guaranteed to genuinely enjoy all that life has to offer.

June 27

"It's in our nature to improve our private selves."

Choosing ways to improve yourself is not the hard part. What's difficult is maintaining the enthusiasm and having the self-discipline to make self-improvement part of your daily routine.

There is no easy way around it. It takes consistent daily effort to get results.

Improving yourself gives you a wonderful sense of satisfaction and feeling of accomplishment that's difficult to match.

Remind yourself every day of the benefits of improving yourself and how these benefits will enhance your life. If you succeed in keeping your awareness high, your enthusiasm will remain high and carry you through.

Start making improvements, today, and don't quit! After all it's part of your nature.

June 28

"Don't be afraid of conflict."

It's natural to become agitated when you face conflict or disagreement. But when you think about it, conflict is a part of life. It's inescapable.

Approaching conflict with a sense of calmness goes a whole lot further in making peace than getting all worked up.

Abandon the concept of winning and losing when facing a disagreement. Instead, think in terms of resolution. Be flexible.

When the other side senses that you're interested in finding a solution, they will be much more agreeable. Rather than confrontation and conflict, you can work together in cooperation to find a solution that suits you both.

June 29

"Why delay your happiness?"

It's not unusual for us to postpone our pleasures and happiness, hoping for a better tomorrow.

Do you place demands on your happiness like, "I'll be happy when I lose 10 pounds," "I'll be happy when I get a new job or new car," "I'll be happy when I find the love of my life?"

Why put off your happiness until Friday night or Sunday morning or this summer or next winter? The real fun in life is the journey - and enjoying the present moment.

If you find yourself placing demands on your happiness, stop! You have a right to enjoy life, right here, right now! As you do, you'll be amazed by the joy of daily life.

June 30

"Attract prosperity."

They say money attracts more money. Wouldn't it be nice to find out? But in truth, prosperity isn't about money anyway. It's about feeling rich in happiness, love and positive experiences.

This is something you not only can have, you can multiply with the right approach.

Appreciate your friends and new friends will arrive. Look for joy each day and you'll find more. Feel happy about all you have in life and you'll find your happiness grows.

Live this way and you'll end up with a wealth of prosperity that all the money in the world can't buy!

July

July 1

"A clear vision is the first step."

A re you happy with how you are living your life? If not, do you have a goals and plans for change?

Having goals makes work and life more interesting, exciting and engaging. Goals help you recognize opportunities when they strike. And, merely because they exist, you are inspired to take action when opportunities present themselves.

Take time to write down what you want and why you want it. Write about your ideal life. What does it look like? Where is it? What are you doing? Who are you with? Describe everything - the place, the people, and most of all how you feel.

Congratulations! You have taken the first step toward clarifying your vision for change.

July 2

"I will be successful, no matter what."

T his is the mantra that successful women live by. They know the secret of success is to believe in themselves and believe in the possibilities. They succeed because they have created a vision for themselves and have taken responsibility for their own future. They refuse to feel like victims or waste time blaming others.

When faced with a challenge, they don't give up. They persevere. They believe they can do whatever it takes to get the job done. They have made peace with the fact that it won't be an easy road and failure may come their way. Instead of giving up, they learn from their failures and keep forging ahead.

This can be your mantra. You are a capable woman and there is no reason you can't use your power of belief to succeed.

Believe in yourself!

July 3

"Let nature perform its magic."

There are times when we feel pressured by life. Deadlines are looming, household appliances suddenly break, we're sleep deprived, or people put unexpected pressures on us. We feel temporarily overwhelmed. We desperately tread water, yet the waves come in relentlessly.

It's time for a mental break!

When your mind is racing or you're close to tears with tiredness and frustration, you need to go within and listen to your inner wisdom. To get in touch with your inner self, seek nature.

Leave the mess that is strewn across the living room floor, walk away from the computer and its ever-amassing emails. Go outside. Do nothing. Consciously become aware of your senses. Listen to the noises around you, feel the surface you are sitting, standing, or lying on, smell the scents and aromas around you, see dispassionately what is before you. Escaping into your primary senses temporarily stops thinking and eases stress.

Leave your inner chaos behind and experience the magic of nature today.

July 4

"Preserve your confidence."

It's so easy to compare yourself to others. When you use others as your measuring stick, you usually come up short. You convince yourself you're not as clever, beautiful, thin or talented.

Lasting satisfaction and confidence comes from appreciating yourself and all that you have to offer. Equating yourself with others eats away at your confidence and leaves you feeling inferior.

Remind yourself of these simple truths. You are a unique and special person, exactly as you are. Your loved ones love you for whom you are. You're one-of-a-kind and you're irreplaceable.

With convictions such as these, your confidence is secure, just as it should be.

July 5

"Be your own unconditional friend."

A re you your own best friend?
Sadly, most women are their own worst enemy. Who needs enemies when you can consult your harshest critic anytime you glance in a mirror? Logically, we should all be our own best friend, but it often isn't the case. We reserve our harshest criticism for ourselves.

Learn now to be gentle with yourself. You deserve special treatment simply because you are special. Who best to comfort you, but you? Who best to compliment you, but you? Learning to love yourself is the greatest gift that you can give yourself. No expensive cosmetics, no retail therapy can deliver the inner warmth of knowing that you are happy being you.

When we love ourselves, it is no longer important that our hair is not perfect or that our thighs are a little dimpled. We don't beat ourselves up for imagined imperfections anymore. In fact, we embrace our imperfections.

Today, look in the mirror and smile. The person there will smile right back. She loves you. Love her, too.

July 6

"Practice being positive."

W e feel so much better when our frame of mind is positive. Negativity is an energy zapper and has no place in our lives.

When you make a conscious decision to let go of pessimistic thoughts, you open up yourself to a whole new life. No longer are you angry at the world or frustrated by your problems.

If you find yourself lamenting over all that is wrong – stop! Choose to focus on all that is right. With this dramatic shift in your attitude you'll be amazed by the good that comes your way.

July 7

"A life without mistakes is lived without joy."

W e fear mistakes more than anything else. Mistakes bring on ridicule. Mistakes expose the unsure, frail and diffident woman hiding within.

Can anyone brag of living a 'mistake-free' life? Perhaps if they were to spend their days on an armchair by the fireside. A life doing this is half-lived, wasted and incomplete.

Fear of making mistakes holds you back from doing many things. Ultimately too many joys go undiscovered. Regrets smother you and you become even more fearful. It's a vicious cycle.

Remember that nobody sits above you. Others may know more, but they have also walked the same path before you. To get to where they are standing, you may have to make a mistake or two. So what, why not feel the joy you deserve and go for it?

July 8

"Claim your personal power."

W hen you are in touch with your personal power, you're confident, decisive, focused, purposeful, energetic and empowered.

Sounds great, but truthfully how often do you feel like this? Personal power or lack of it is created by you and you alone. You decrease your power by blaming others or external forces for your misfortunes. Why give up what is rightfully yours?

Claim your personal power today! Try not to blame outside forces for disappointments. Don't wait for others to change their behavior, instead choose to change your response. Stand strong and refuse to be a victim. You can do it!

July 9

"A life consistent with your values
makes you secure, confident and strong."

What do you believe in? What do you stand for? In other words, what are your values?

Values lie at the very heart of all you do as a woman, because values create the core of your personality and character. Only when your values are clear and you honor them, can you experience consistent self-confidence and self-esteem.

Think about what's important to you. Ask yourself, "What do I value?" "To what do I aspire?" and even "What do I despise?" Honest answers to these questions make you secure, confident and strong.

Do you live a life consistent with your values? If not, make changes until you can answer, "Yes!"

July 10

"You have a choice."

Every day you make literally hundreds of choices, consciously and unconsciously. One of those choices is your attitude. What was your attitude like when you woke up? What is it like now?

When you're aware of how your attitude affects your well-being, choices are so much easier to make. With this new found knowledge, you can literally change whatever you can dream of.

You deserve a great life, happiness and self-fulfillment. Choose today to make it that way!

July 11

"Pain is followed by joy."

Every woman knows something about what it feels like to be dumped, divorced or jilted. It's almost like losing a limb.

The pain may be deeper if a woman has been innocent enough to miss the vital signs. Divorce, adultery or even death – women feel it so strong as to be shattered by the impact.

It's important for you to realize that life DOES go on!

There is no dramatic pause in life. When the boat rocks and disaster strikes, no doubt there is pain. Everybody needs time to get over their misery.

But inevitably, your future has to go on. One has to let go of the agonies of the past and step into a new dawn. New interests, new projects, new faces, and new horizons have to be found.

After a period of mourning and bereavement, when you feel ready to go on, MOVE AHEAD – confidently and purposefully. This new turn in your life may not be joyful at first. But the heart has a way of making old wounds seem less painful if you're willing to let go.

After a while these new facets will give you immense joy, once again!

July 12

"There is a princess inside every woman."

When a girl is young, she carries her dreams in her twinkling eyes. She is convinced that there is a princess, a very attractive princess, living inside her.

With time she becomes sober and gets enmeshed in the realities of day-to-day life. Slowly that little princess becomes a distant memory. Then, one day, even the memory vanishes.

A time comes when she scoffs at the idea that a princess is within her. What? A princess living inside this straggly, gangly, fat, shabbily-dressed, pale frame? Not possible!

That's where she's wrong. That princess still lives inside her.

However, she is buried underneath the pile of worries, pain and misery. She can be freed if you believe and search for her within you.

So, turn back the clock. Remember that little girl who used to look into the mirror and dream wonderful dreams? Become that girl again.

Don't allow the present to kill the beauty within you. You are still that strong, independent, joyful human being you left behind. The little princess within you has just lost her way. Help her come back.

July 13

"Every woman is work in progress."

When you commit yourself to continuous improvement, you can't help but feel better about yourself. With growth comes the willingness to take risks and accept challenges. It's exciting because there is always something new you can be, do, have and learn.

It is in this reaching that you find out who you really are and all that you are capable of. And, as a result, you evolve as a human being.

As you build momentum, you'll shine with confidence and inspire others along the way. Now, that's what progress is all about!

July 14

"Your emotions are your messengers."

To be true to yourself and to those around you, it's a must to learn to manage your emotions. It is a critical step toward living a happy, successful and fulfilled life. This doesn't mean that you control them by ignoring them or repressing them, it simply means listening to them. What are they telling you?

When you let your emotions control you, you miss the message that they carry. When you ignore them for fear of what they might cause you to do or feel, they simply return as anger later.

Observe your self-talk as your emotions peak and fall. Tune in and identify any judgments you might have about the way you feel. These thoughts translate into what you believe to be true about yourself. They can be accurate or untrue and damaging. You decide if change is in order.

July 15

"Keep the passion for change alive."

When you decide to change something in your life you start out with commitment, determination and passion to make it happen. But, as time passes the euphoria that dominated your thoughts has a way of waning.

If you let your passion completely fizzle out, the commitment you made becomes internalized as failure. You feel like you let yourself down. Your self-esteem and self-confidence sink. Don't let this happen!

Realize it is up to you and nobody else to stay motivated. Dig deep within your being and keep pushing to reach your goal. It's up to you to keep the passion fire alive and you can do it.

Right now is the time to go the extra mile. You have come such a long way - now is not the time to quit!

July 16

"The present is where it's at."

How much of your life do you spend living in the present? Research shows that it's very little. We spend a lot of time ruminating about the past or speculating about the future. To make things worse, much of this "non-present" thinking is negative. We think about the things we might have done, or we think about future dramas that may, in reality, never occur. Or, we might just simply wish it was Friday and effectively wish a significant portion of our lives away.

The secret to real peace and happiness is to live in the present - to focus on the "Now."

If you catch yourself living in another time zone remember, the present is where fulfillment is.

July 17

"Take charge of chaos."

Do you sometimes feel like you're living a life of chaos; chasing your tail with no relief in sight?

Are you in a state where everything takes longer and requires more effort than you thought? Do you want to be organized, but haven't got the time to clear up the mess? Are the words "free time" not in your vocabulary?

Stop for a moment and consider living by the motto, "Don't put off till tomorrow what can be done today."

If you start today by organizing your desk, your closet, your garage, anything that's in chaos, the reward is less time spent finding things, less frustration and less stress.

With just a couple of changes, you'll feel in control and recoup lost time and energy. Chaos will start to subside and ultimately you'll have time for the things you enjoy. Try it!

July 18

"Our friendships mirror ourselves."

You can't choose your family, but you can choose your friends. So, how helpful are your friends to self-growth?

Are they supportive, encouraging you to strive and achieve? Do they provide a sanctuary of love and warmth when the world becomes cold and bitter? Do you love them with all your heart and is that love reciprocated?

Or, are your "friends" not really friends at all? Is there a tinge of jealousy when you succeed? In hard times are they unavailable, only to reappear once the crisis is past? Do they spend their time with you talking in negative ways about others?

If your friendship experience is the former, then you are indeed blessed. If it is the latter, now is the time to take stock of the negativity that you are allowing into your life.

Release your relationships with negative, draining people. Choose friends wisely and you're life with be filled with love.

July 19

"Cease to be a victim."

W asting energy worrying about what the laws of the universe are delivering to your neighbor only leads to frustration and resentment.

Instead, accept how the law of cause and effect influences your own life, your relationships, successes and disappointments. It's much more satisfying to be engaged in your own destiny, rather than the lives of others.

You have control over your own life, so concentrate on that. Knowing you are in the driver's seat guarantees peace of mind.

July 20

"Star stuff."

A stronomer Carl Sagan said that we're all made of "star-stuff." Whatever it is that we are made of; we are certainly made of the same "stuff" - the same atoms, molecules and cells. We are much more alike than we realize.

Remembering this can help calm you, center you, and give you a sense of connectedness - both with the universe and with others.

Try this experiment today. With each person that you pass, become aware that the "stuff" - the essence – what's inside you is inside them. Check out the person in the car coming toward you. You both share the same essential life essence. The people on the subway, on the bus, at your office - all are made of the same unique, special, and mysterious "stuff" as you.

After a day of literally "connecting" in your mind with every person you encounter, you will find your mood is buoyant. You will feel part of a bigger world than the one you normally inhabit. Seeing yourself in others and others in you, brings calmness, peace and an incredible sense of belonging.

July 21

"Refuse to remain in your comfort zone."

Your comfort zone feels safe, familiar and relaxing. The problem is, if you're spending too much time there you may not be growing and evolving as a woman.

It takes a tremendous amount of bravery to do what is unfamiliar and uncomfortable. The good news is, the payoff is worth it. Your self-esteem rises and your self-confidence becomes unyielding.

Challenge yourself this week. Put yourself in an uncomfortable situation on purpose. How about volunteering for a project that you would normally shy away from? Strike up a conversation with a stranger or sign up for a class to learn something new.

Whatever step you take, expect to be uncomfortable, but know in your heart that you're doing wonders for your well-being.

July 22

"Frame your thoughts with awareness."

It's no secret that we have the ability to program ourselves to believe and act in negative ways. The good news is that we're also blessed with the ability to program ourselves to believe and act in positive ways.

The starting point is awareness.

You must first become familiar with how your thoughts make you feel and act. Ask yourself, what thoughts make me feel happy, sad, jealous, mad, etc.? How do I react to my feelings? Once you have the answers to these questions, consider yourself aware.

When you're in touch with your feelings you're consciously able to program yourself for positive action. Next time you catch yourself in a thought that doesn't feel good, stop, and consciously choose to react in another way. When you re-frame your thinking, everything changes.

July 23

"The power of enthusiasm works like a magnet."

The more excited you are about accomplishing something important to you, the more excited others will be about helping out. Enthusiastic emotions are contagious.

Many great women committed to worthy causes are full of enthusiasm. Their infectious excitement naturally attracts the help and support of others.

The more passion you have for your life and activities, the more charisma and enthusiasm you will communicate. These two traits draw people to you like magnets.

Use the power of your enthusiasm and watch how effortlessly you attract the support of others into your life.

July 24

"Clean your spirit."

When our mothers told us to clean our rooms, they were unwittingly giving us a gift that would have lasting repercussions. Although we grumbled when asked for the umpteenth time to clear the mess, we were actually doing more than physically cleaning our rooms. We were cleaning our spirits as well.

There is a spiritual side to everything - even household chores. Cluttered rooms are often indicative of a cluttered mind. Messy houses may point to messy lives. If you are feeling overwhelmed by life, go clean a closet. It's the quickest and cheapest therapy for regaining a sense of control and a feeling of accomplishment.

From that platform of confidence, you can then go on to solve the more difficult aspects of your life, knowing that you have solidarity and order backing you up.

Cleaning a closet, a room, or an entire house can give you a real sense of power. It's like saying to the universe: "My house is in order!"

July 25

"Welcome change."

There is nothing more certain in our lives than change. Yet many of us fear change and make elaborate plans to avoid it. We fear the new and find comfort in the stability of the known and familiar.

But to grow, you need to not only accept change, but to embrace it, joyfully. Think of a flowing stream as representing your life. In some places it flows smoothly, with barely a ripple as it travels on its journey. At other places along the way, obstacles create great turbulence; the water roars and thunders as it crashes through gorges and down steep falls. These represent both the easy and difficult times your experience.

Yet, a stream may have a place where the water becomes banked up, stagnant, unhealthy. Here, nothing thrives and nothing changes.

Welcome the rushing waters of change into your life, for change means growth, spiritual health, and self-realization. Embrace each new direction you encounter with courage and enthusiasm. It's the key to a happier you.

July 26

"Follow the roadmap of life."

The best way to achieve your goal is to have one in the first place!

As obvious as it sounds, there are plenty of people who have no real goal in life. When asked, they'll answer that their aim is to "be happy." But what does that really mean?

To achieve what you want in life, you need to set goals. If you don't have direction, you have nothing to aim for. Without a target, you are shooting blanks into the wind. Real desires are solid, not nebulous and vague. How can you hope to achieve if you have nothing to shoot for?

Be definite! Set well-defined goals. As you do, you will discover a map to a better life. It doesn't matter if these goals are small, at first. They are still goals, and when you achieve them, you can move onto the next one with a sense of confidence.

Set an achievable goal, today, and relish journeying toward your destination!

July 27

"Give yourself praise."

Why do we find it so hard to praise ourselves when we achieve something? It doesn't seem to matter whether our accomplishments are small or sensational. Giving ourselves a pat on the back for a job well done can be the emotional equivalent of climbing Mt. Everest!

Perhaps you were trained to be modest, perhaps you were told you were hopeless and you didn't learn to believe in yourself. Perhaps your past achievements were simply ignored by your parents and mentors and you've simply given up expecting accolades.

We often freely praise others for their achievements yet withhold it from ourselves. But self-praise is important, even more important than praise from others, because you can't always depend on praise and recognition from others. The ability to self-praise is essential in building healthy self-esteem.

Today, begin the journey of self-commendation. Praise yourself for each achievement, however insignificant you may think it is. Watch yourself achieving as you go about your day. And give yourself a pat on the back - you deserve it.

July 28

"Breathe like a baby."

When we are stressed, we often breathe from the upper chest instead of down into our lower lungs. Take note of your breathing. If your shoulders rise and fall, then you are a shallow breather. This way of breathing spells "stress."

Lie down and place you hand on your belly. Breathe in so that you can feel your belly rise and fall. This is the way a baby breathes.

When women are pregnant, they often instinctively place their hand on their belly. It is an age-old behavior for protecting the infant within. Use the same technique to protect your own inner child. Guard the peace and serenity of your inner child as you would a real baby.

By placing your hand on your belly at regular intervals during the day you will encourage better breathing habits and release your stress.

July 29

"Release what needs to be free."

It's really hard to let go - especially for us women. For many, it is almost instinctive to cling. Whether it's a love letter, a secure job, a relationship, or a dear friend - holding on to what is no longer ours only causes pain.

When you let go of old things, you pave the way for new things - experiences that are perhaps more exciting, adventurous or wholesome. When you let go of the past, you free yourself. When you let go of that which is rotting and decaying, you are then ready to embrace the fresh, unopened buds of change.

Have the courage to let go. When you relinquish the past, your future embraces you.

July 30

"Take a chance."

Ever felt embarrassed after someone rebuffed your invitation to go for coffee? Ever felt hurt when you opened yourself up to another person and they didn't react the way that you had hoped? Ever felt scared for any number of reasons?

Congratulations! You're alive. And growing, too! If we never take a chance, if we never stretch ourselves, there are two things that we can be sure of. One is that we will never feel hurt or embarrassed or scared. The other is that we will stagnate. Safe in our comfort zone, we will find in time that comfort zone has become a prison. We have dealt ourselves a life sentence of "safety." Yet safety equals stagnation.

Be embarrassed! Be hurt! Be frightened! The rewards of growth and change are permanently rewarding. Slowly, through taking chances on people and situations, we mold ourselves into the person we want to be. We grow. We learn. We change for the better. The end result outweighs the temporary pain encountered on the journey.

Take a chance on life today.

July 31

"The fewer rules the better."

When it comes to the rules you have about how life should be or how other people should behave, the less you have, the easier it is to be happy. Why? Because, when you cease to impose unrealistic expectations on people and on life, you not only reduce the likelihood of disappointment, you also let go of unnecessary stresses and false demands.

Instead of always trying to channel life, ease up and go with the flow. Enjoy what comes your way. Try your hardest to accept people as they are and try not to force them into your own mold - celebrate their individual differences.

Greet life's surprises with joy and excitement and you'll end up with a more fulfilling life than was ever written in the rules!

August

August 1

"Collect your fruit."

Sometimes we get so busy doing all the tasks we need to do each day in our roles as women, partners, mothers, daughters and workers, that we forget to collect our winnings. We put in all the groundwork - we clean, we cook, we work, we care for, we discipline - but we get so bogged down with these necessities that we neglect to grow.

We need to remember that our spiritual life requires us to stretch ourselves and reach out to claim our full potential. The actor Will Rogers once said, "Why not go out on a limb? That's where the fruit is." Think about that statement for a moment.

Often we spend much of our lives on groundwork. In planting terms, we dig, we sow, we water, we fertilize. Yet sometimes we forget the most important task. And that is to dust off our metaphorical ladders and reach out to collect the fruit of our labors.

Take time to go out on a limb today – and gather your well-deserved fruit!

August 2

"It's just one of those days."

There will be days when you'll end up having a melt down, freaking out, and going into an emotional tailspin. It's completely normal. The key is to let it happen.

What's important is, once it's over, you need to pick up the pieces and regain your composure. This is your responsibility. It's crucial not to beat yourself up because you lost control. Remember a fall out doesn't mean failure.

Expect bad days every once in a while. These days may scare and upset you, but realize they are all part of life.

A great day is just around the corner!

August 3

"Your beliefs determine your prosperity."

Women who believe money is the only measure of prosperity are likely to spend their lives falling short. Conversely, those who see prosperity in terms of wealth of happiness, tend to believe their lives are full of riches, which in itself attracts more and more.

Today, take stock of what you have in your life. Instead of focusing on what you don't have, put your attention to the rewards you have already received and those that are all around you waiting to be appreciated.

Reflect on your loved ones, your surroundings and your talents - for you are prosperous indeed.

August 4

"A list can be a lifesaver."

Feeling overloaded by work and responsibilities? Confused by all the tasks that keep going round and round in your head? Do you find it impossible to effectively use the time you have available now?

The solution? Make a list of everything you need to do in the next 24 hours. Make sure you divide your list into what has to be done and what could be done, if time permits.

Many people underestimate the value of lists. Sure, the act of writing a list of chores doesn't get them done. But, it does get them down on paper and out of that merry-go-round operating in your mind.

Seeing your tasks as words on a page allows you to take control of your thinking - to plan, to undertake, and most importantly, to cross them off in triumph as they are achieved.

The locus of control is back in your hands. You become calmer and able to work more efficiently. You learn not to fear times of overload.

Start practicing your list-making, today.

August 5

"Don't expect your partner to fulfill all your needs."

It's unfair to expect your partner to be able and willing to render all your needs, no one person can do that. Though it may feel easy and less risky, it's unfair.

Reach out in earnest to others in your life for fulfillment. You'll probably find that different friends and family members are more than willing to share their expertise.

One may have a great sense of humor, another a great listener and another a financial whiz. When you have many friends and relatives in your network you take the pressure off your partner and ultimately you both are happier.

August 6

"Women with high self-esteem feel terrific about themselves."

Your self-esteem is probably the most important part of your personality. It dictates your performance in almost everything you do. The amount of self-esteem you have determines your levels of vitality, enthusiasm and attraction.

To be your best and to feel amazing, you should always be in a state of self-esteem building and maintenance. Just as you take responsibility for your level of physical fitness, you need to take responsibility for your self-esteem.

Self-esteem building is not easy. It takes effort and perseverance, but if you're willing to make the effort, you'll be rewarded with a gracious life.

August 7

"The special gift of a mother."

Women have the sensitivity to love their children unconditionally and under any circumstances, even when their children disappoint them. What a gift!

There is no love in the world more absolute than a mother's love for her child. No matter what your children do, you want to protect them. It doesn't matter what mistakes they make, you believe they can still get it right.

What a gift you are to the world. By being steadfast and unconditional in your love, you help your children recover from their mistakes and gain the courage to face future hurdles.

You give them the strength and tenacity to become some of the world's most valuable adults - just like you knew they would.

August 8

"Winning isn't everything, but wanting to is."

Perseverance is the golden key to being successful in anything you do. Be it losing weight, improving your relationships, or even starting a business. It's a matter of hanging on long after others have quit.

Perseverance overcomes almost everything. When you fall, perseverance tells you to get up. When you're defeated, perseverance tells you to try again. When you feel like quitting, perseverance doesn't let you.

If at first you don't succeed, try, try, try again. Therein lies the secret to being a winner.

August 9

"Qualities you see in others,
reveals something about you."

You may not realize it, but the characteristics you like or dislike in others delivers a special message.

If you respond to a person that you see as outgoing, positive and energetic, these are most likely qualities you possess, but have not fully embraced or developed. Likewise, if you react to the overbearing nature of another, then do a self-check, you may have the tendency to be overbearing yourself.

Either way, tune into what you do and don't admire in others. Take note of your emotional response. With this new found awareness you can't help but discover something you didn't know about yourself.

August 10

"Discouragement steals your dreams."

Hand-in-hand with setbacks and challenges comes discouragement. Its ferocity can stop you in your tracks and before you know it your dreams seem unreachable. Stop! This is only true if you give in.

Today is the day you will conquer discouragement. Today is the day you will feel more determined and stronger than ever. Today is the day you will put one foot in front of the other and persevere.

Make a commitment to yourself that you will never give up when you feel disheartened, but rather, you will view these feelings as a sign to work harder.

You're entitled to your dreams and aspirations. So why not make this commitment today?

August 11

"Mistakes are opportunities."

Making mistakes are an integral part of living, learning and growing as a human being. We all make them!

The question is, what do you do after the blunder? As a child, if you were made to feel like a failure, you most likely believe you're inadequate and often give up. If you were told that mistakes were inevitable and you were encouraged to try harder the next time, you probably have a better attitude.

If you feel depleted and defeated after making a mistake, make up your mind today to change your mindset. Realize that mistakes are lessons in disguise. They're your chance to achieve better results the next time armed with knowledge you didn't have before.

August 12

"Happiness is abundant in the joy of achievement."

Happiness doesn't come from successfully completing simple or mundane tasks, it comes from completing a task that demands your best efforts.

When you pour your heart and soul into something and you accomplish that something, the afterglow of satisfaction you feel is happiness. It is the thrill of all your efforts and hard work.

Each and every one of us needs to accomplish, achieve and triumph to be happy. Our human spirit requires it. Remember that happiness thrives in activity and accomplishment. Go for it!

August 13

"A brilliant conversationalist talks to you about you."

Most of us are never happier than when the conversation has turned away from others and toward ourselves. When people talk to us about our lives, our family, our achievements, or our goals, we subconsciously feel we must be worthy of attention. Our confidence rises; we feel energized, cared about, and uplifted. Deep inside we're a little proud that we have become the center of attention.

Now think about how little it would take from you to create all those positive feelings in others! A few questions, a focused ear, and a genuine interest in what you are hearing, and you too can pass on the gift of added energy, caring and confidence to a friend, a neighbor, or a family member. Imagine the power we could create if we all did this today! Let's try it!

August 14

"Decisions require your instinct and intuition."

When you're faced with a decision, your instinct and intuition are just as important as experience. Trusting your intuition allows you to recognize and seize opportunities more quickly than those who waste time and momentum examining every angle. Your intuition also keeps decisions from becoming overwhelming.

Think of a situation when you ignored your "gut feeling." It may have been when you hired someone, dealings with clients, or even trusting a friend. Whatever it may be, you probably learned a valuable lesson about intuition at one time or another.

Remember, with every opportunity there is a right moment to take action toward a certain purpose. Trust your intuition and be ready to capture the moment. You won't be let down.

August 15

"Build an internal retreat for peace."

Use your imagination to build a personal sanctuary. A place you can go for centering. A hideaway to refocus your attention and attitude.

Begin by imagining a favorite place, a relaxing and private place where you can enjoy being alone. Perhaps it's a tropical beach, a bench in the back yard, or even a luxurious hotel room. Place yourself in this place and notice how you feel. Are you relaxed, calmer and more secure? Let these feelings sink into your core and feel the soothing relaxing peace of your solitude.

Your retreat is always there for you. If you're feeling tired, stressed or unable to cope, use your mind's eye to go to your special place.

It will change your day.

August 16

"Life is full of distractions."

Does it seem like something or someone is always trying to steer you off track? You have a point of focus, an objective, or destination, then something comes along that captures your attention and points you in an entirely different direction.

Of course a certain amount of distraction can't be avoided. The good news is there is something you can do to deal with these diversions and get back to being productive. The best solution is to simply accept them as inevitable, give them the attention they deserve, and then get back to the task at hand as quickly as possible.

Don't let distractions upset you or derail your best intentions. Remember that an emotional reaction is likely to cost you far more time and energy than the distraction itself.

August 17

"A lesson from the lawn."

Imagine if a blade of grass decided it had had enough. It was done with having its head snipped off every weekend and its seeds - its future - cut off in their prime. Who could blame it?

Yet, what does that ol' blade of grass do? It doesn't say: "I give up! I'm getting nowhere!" It just keeps on growing. It continually takes in the energy from the sunlight and magically converts carbon dioxide from the air into food to make more leaves and more seeds.

A blade of grass is resilient.

You too, can learn to be as resilient as the grass. You may be cut down on a regular basis, yet your strength is in standing up, dusting yourself off, and starting all over again. Even when grass is covered in concrete, it finds a way to grow up through the cracks.

And, so must you.

Take a "leaf" out of the grass' book. Connect with your own resilience and keep on growing.

August 18

"Happiness is wanting what you have, not having what you want."

At first glance this sounds like the same thing, take a closer look, it's not.

If you're completely fulfilled by spending time with your friends and family because you really want to be with them, then you truly want what you have.

On the flip side, if you drive the nicest car and have a huge house, and have worked hard to get those things, then you've been successful at having what you want.

When you have what you want eventually the feeling of satisfaction wears off. Once you get what you want the old wants are replaced by new wants and the cycle continues. True happiness remains at bay.

Look around you, happiness may be closer than you think. It may just be a matter of changing what you value.

August 19

"Discomfort is a small price to pay for growth."

Many women find it difficult to say "No." So they keep saying "Yes."

Some women hurt when they hear praise. They shake their heads and deny their worth.

Many women resist love. They are the caregivers, but they are afraid to be taken care of.

Sometimes a woman wants to get intimate, but she is held back by shame.

Fear, shame and doubt eat away at your self-esteem. Today, decide the course YOU want to take. Don't always feel compelled to flow with the current.

Say "No" firmly and loudly when you need to. When someone praises you, smile gently, yet proudly. Allow yourself to be loved and cared for. Take control of your intimate moments by deciding and expressing what YOU want.

Allow discomfort to wash over you and fade away. Do the things that you REALLY want and throw away the mask that has been hiding you. You can do it!

August 20

"How beautiful do you think you are?"

When you look in the mirror what do you see? Do you look only at flaws? Your big nose, your double chin, or perhaps your not so perfect skin?

Every woman has her own self-proclaimed list of flaws. We're all guilty.

Did you know the more you focus on your flaws the less you see your perfections? Your perfections can be seen in the mirror too!

Why not consider your positive attributes - your perfect lips, your beautiful eyes, your shiny hair, and your fantastic smile?

Accept who you are and what you have and leave perfection behind.

You're a beautiful woman!

August 21

"It's never too late to improve your brain power."

Mental work-outs keep you alert, active and able to deal better with problems. They'll help you ward off burn-out and they're guaranteed to keep life interesting.

There are hundreds of ways to challenge your intellect. Learning to play an instrument involves senses of touch, sight and sound. Music requires you to translate symbols requiring you to plan ahead and challenge your motor skills.

You can even try using your non dominant hand. If you brush your hair with your right hand, try your left. There are always

crossword puzzles, scrabble and chess. And if you're really
ambitious, learn a new language.

Take your brain to the gym and give it a workout! You'll have
fun, feel like you're challenging yourself and maybe even make a
new friend.

August 22

"It all starts with the voice inside."

When your self-talk is positive, it can cheer you up when
things go wrong, encourage you when you want to say
"No," and deepen relationships when you're unsure. You may
not be aware of it, but your subconscious voice is always sending
you messages. You talk to yourself all day long. Do you know
what your inner voice is saying?

Now, is the time to listen and learn. When you recognize
what's going on in the privacy of your mind, you can change
negative thoughts to positive ones. Take charge of your thoughts.
It is the beginning of both wisdom and happiness.

August 23

"Enthusiasm where the fun is."

When enthusiasm strikes, you know because you want to
jump up and down and scream with happiness. It's a
moment where your heart soars because you have just felt or
done something that inspires you deep within.

Enthusiasm is where your body screams with excitement and
you hear that "Yes!!!" from deep inside. It's one of the best
feelings in the world.

Today, no matter what your rational mind says look and listen
for the places, events, ideas, people and activities that make your
heart shout a loud "Yes!!!" Next, spend some time deciding how
to bring more of those things into your life.

Make a commitment to yourself to do the things you need to do
to live a more enthusiastic life. When you're enthusiastic you

look forward to each and every day. And, that's what makes life
so fun!

August 24

"When facing something new, act like a child."

When children try something new they practice over and
over until they master it. They make the challenge of
learning fun and the work of training turns into play.

Unlike a child's mind your adult mind reminds you of the
reasons why you can't do something, which creates resistance
and ultimately leads to quitting. You end up turning back to your
old ways, to comfort zones that have nothing new to offer.
Imagine yourself as a child. Now, how do you feel about that new
project?

Next time you tackle something new, adopt the mindset of a
child. Remain open and try not to place expectations on the
outcome. Before you know it, you will be immersed in continual
positive reinforcement. Success will come easily because you are
thinking like a child!

August 25

"Happiness is not the destination."

Many women slog for a lifetime looking for happiness.
They feel guilty doing things they enjoy. So they take
care of their jobs, their families, their children, and their pets
thinking that the time for happiness will come later. In the end,
they discover that it doesn't.

Believe that you DESERVE happiness right now!

You know those early hours in the morning when the house is
quiet and the mist is floating outside the window? THAT is
happiness. Remember how it felt to hold your baby for the first
time? THAT is happiness. Remember how you felt when you
achieved what seemed like an impossible goal? THAT is
happiness.

Do not defer your happiness to a later date. Find joy in what you do every day.

August 26

"Step aside world, here I come."

The world will step aside for a woman with clearly defined objectives and a strong desire to attain them.

No matter what your plan is to launch yourself toward success, the time to start is now. Not tomorrow, not next week, or next month - now!

Don't waste another day waiting for all the right conditions. There will never be a perfect time to get started. The important thing is to take that first step and get started immediately!

Proceed with determination and don't let fear, doubt or others stop you. Your path will become clear as you move forward.

August 27

"The best career is one with meaning."

To be truly happy in your career you need to find the right kind of work for you. Not something you think you should do or something somebody else wants you to do.

Some women like to lead, others prefer to follow, some are independent, and others prefer to be part of a team. There is no right or wrong. Ask yourself, "What feels right for me?" "How can I use my unique and natural talents?" "How can I bring out the best in myself and provide it to others as a service?"

Dare to take the steps toward finding your own true path by answering the questions above. You'll discover what comes naturally and what activities make you the happiest.

Best of all, you'll feel genuine satisfaction and pride when you spend your days doing something you value.

August 28

"Your mind can shatter your limits."

You have a choice. You can be confident or unconfident, happy or unhappy, attractive or unattractive, powerful or weak.

All these things start with you and what you tell yourself about what you can and cannot do.

Your mind is where you define your limits. If your inner thoughts are self-defeating, you will become what they tell you. If your thoughts are empowering, positive and upbeat, you will become that woman. It's a self-fulfilling prophecy.

Impress upon your mind what you want to be, not what you don't want to be.

That is where the true power of self- suggestion lies.

August 29

"Take care of you!"

If you live inside an out-of-control schedule, like trying to cram three days of work into one, the personal toll is high. Undoubtedly, your stress levels are high and you feel overwhelmed.

It's okay to slow down and pace yourself. The truth is you'll accomplish more if you set a reasonable pace; one that you can maintain for the long run.

Don't forget to schedule time to relax and refresh your body, soul and spirit. Dinner with friends, a long walk, or even a relaxing bubble bath will do wonders in letting go and grounding yourself.

You deserve balance in your life. It's up to you to make it happen.

August 30

"Respect drives success."

The process of setting challenging goals and then writing out a plan to achieve them causes you to feel much more confident about achieving your dreams and consequently better about yourself.

You gain self-respect as you move step-by-step toward the completion of something that is important to you. It really is the key to success! It's SO important to have clear plans for the changes you want to make in your life and to earnestly work toward realizing them.

Each progressive step you take toward reaching your goals is like a stepping stone of "like" and "self-respect." You feel more positive and accomplished which fuels all your endeavors.

Take that step today!

August 31

"Action, not perfection, creates results."

When you start something new, don't worry about doing it perfectly, initially. Just start and recognize that adjustments will need to be made along the way. In other words, take action!

It's easier to take action when you don't expect perfection. Obstacles don't intimidate you and adjustments are seen as part of the learning process. Expect them and be ready to reach into your tool bag for a solution at any moment.

Action, even imperfect action, will bring results, and eventually, perfection may follow.

September

September 1

"Reality is something to rise above."

Great things are accomplished when you believe that what's inside of you is superior to your circumstances. Believing you're more important than any of your problems, that you're bigger than anything that can happen to you, takes courage.

You may have to dig deep for this courage, but it is there. Rise above fear and doubt. Remind yourself that you are in control, that the time to live is today!

September 2

"When your values are reflected in your life, your self-esteem shows it."

Having clear standards and values to which you are committed makes getting through life much easier. With a foundation like this, you never second-guess yourself. You always know you're doing what you believe in and what is best for you.

Women that know and practice their beliefs have high levels of self-esteem and confidence. They are comfortable with who they are and the purpose of their lives.

The more clearly defined your values and ideals, the more committed you are to living up to them. Take stock of your values. Are you living a life that reflects them? If not, you know what to do!

September 3

"Never give up on a dream."

Patience and persistence make dreams come true. It's easy to get frustrated and impatient while working hard to achieve dreams that still seem far away. When you get that inkling to give up, remember this old saying.

"Winners never quit and quitters never win!"

The positive energy you create paves the way for your dreams to come true. Just when you think you've exhausted all possibilities, you'll find another way, a better way - and more importantly, another day to live your dreams.

September 4

"There are many ways to know yourself."

You are a multifaceted person. Discovering yourself can be the adventure of a lifetime. Learning how comfortable or uncomfortable you are in certain situations, if you're outgoing or quiet, what makes you happy or sad, and knowing what you're good at and what you're not, is part of nurturing a balanced life. Do you know all those things about yourself? Or, are you too busy, too stressed, or too focused on someone else to care?

Knowing as much as you can about yourself makes decision-making easier. When you know "you," it's easier to ensure that your choices are the right ones. This knowledge is your key to harmony and balance. So, take the time to know yourself. It's the only way to make certain that you live a happy, fulfilling life.

September 5

"Collect Happiness."

We all experience days when we feel spiritually depleted - we feel down, uncared for, unloved. The world is not our oyster today. Yet, like many of our impressions, this, is an illusion. We are the same yesterday, today and tomorrow, even though circumstances may try to persuade us otherwise.

This is when we need the comfort of a "Happy Box." Take the time to make one for yourself and you will reap the benefits over and over. Fill your box with items that you have collected over time: a special card from a favorite aunt, your child's first attempt to write "I love you," a photo of you and your best friend. That pretty stone you found on holiday, your child's first tooth, the ribbon off a bunch of flowers from a caring friend; all help you to re-align your spirit and see the world as the wonder that it is.

Your "Happy Box" represents tangible items of the love and joy that are present in your world each and every day. It's like money in the bank of happiness. Start your account today.

September 6

"A choice is not really a choice, until you act upon it."

If you decide to act on your best beliefs, then don't follow through - you are buying into "indecision."

Indecision and procrastination are what we do to avoid the responsibility of putting our choices into action. If you find yourself always in a state of indecision, perhaps you are trying to do too much and need to break things down into smaller digestible steps. Perhaps your decision is not in line with your values or some important aspect of your life. You may need to reevaluate what you're trying to do.

Remember that you will never know if a decision is right or wrong until it's acted upon. Every important decision involves risk and sometimes tradeoffs. If you have a decision to make, make it today. And, more importantly, act on it today.

September 7

"Your hopes and dreams are always alive within you."

As you grow older you've probably found that your childhood hopes and dreams haven't materialized. Instead, coping with the problems of everyday living has replaced those dreams. Schedules and responsibilities have fogged your vision.

Now is the time to look back at your childhood ambitions and find the inner strength and courage to make them realities. Maybe not every single ambition you once had, but at least one or two that really matter.

It's never too late to make your hopes and dreams come true. You may have to work hard, but if you are persistent and press past the wall of doubt, you will be successful!

September 8

"Holding grudges will consume your emotional energy, if you let it."

Holding grudges uses lots of emotional energy. And, when your emotional energy is tied up in a grudge, it holds you in the past. Grudges hold energy hostage and it's not until you forgive that your energy can be restored.

Think of forgiveness as something you do for yourself. Think of it as something that makes you stronger, not weaker.

If you're holding grudges, let them go. Seek reconciliation if needed. If you find it hard to forgive then start with the small grudges and work your way up. The physical feeling of relief and the energy reclaimed will be well worth it.

Forgive today. It's time to move on!

September 9

"Every job has built in difficulties."

Difficulties alone don't cause job burnout. It's the lack of control that drains us and leads to frustration. If people and situations don't demand our best, we soon become bored. So, some stress is both expected and good.

To avoid job burnout, we must embrace challenges that keep us interested and performing at our peak. Labeling difficulties as challenges also helps us balance our personal and work related lives.

You have a personal responsibility to yourself, your well-being, and your happiness. Don't let job stress control you. If you need to make changes to avoid burnout, take action today!

September 10

"Planning brings your future into the present."

It isn't enough to sit on the sidelines and hope for things to get better. You've got to ask yourself, "What steps am I going to take to get the things in life I want?" Achieving great goals takes planning and your life is no different.

Take charge! Make plans to bridge the distance between where you are now and the future you can see so clearly. Define, clarify and implement your plans. If you need help, don't be bashful. Ask someone for it. You will be surprised how willing others are to help you succeed.

Remember, your plan is your path and your guide. No woman with a plan has ever lost her way on the road to her goals!

September 11

"Recap and thank yourself."

After each day, it's important to review what you've done and give yourself a pat on the back. It's okay to bask in well-deserved praise, to dwell, for a moment, on your hard won accomplishments.

Remember, motivation begins with appreciation. Once you acknowledge the things that you are doing right, it's easy to feel motivated to try harder, tomorrow.

Gratitude is a great way to build those internal fires of achievement. So, be proud of the fruits of your efforts and thank yourself for a job well done!

September 12

"Change the way you think and you will change the way you feel."

B reaking the habit of negative thinking and replacing it with an "I can and I will" attitude is the change called for by inner confidence.

Negative thinking can be so interwoven in the fabric of whom you are that it is natural to assume it's normal. It's not! Breaking the cycle of negative thinking means you must acknowledge and face your harsh inner critic.

You have strengths, skills and talents. Recognizing and believing in them is what confidence is all about. When you are confident, it's easy to feel great, because your inner critic becomes your inner champion!

September 13

"There is nothing positive about being a worry wart."

D o you worry too much?
       Some worrying is good. It warns us of error and helps with decision-making. But if you find yourself worrying all the time, you are robbing yourself of precious energy and happy hours.

When you worry, your body tenses, your mind races, and your heart stresses. Focusing on negative future outcomes or past failures is an unhealthy way to spend your time.

Resolve to regain this lost energy. Focus on today and handle things as they occur. Know that what's happened in the past is water under the bridge. Remember that what may happen in the future is, for the most part, out of your control. Live happily in the "here and now." It's the only way to thrive!

September 14

"With balance comes contentment."

Are you pressured by juggling all the different roles in life? Are you feeling overwhelmed by the competing demands on you? If so, it's time to reassess your priorities and bring things back into perspective.

When your well-being is forced to take a back seat, burnout becomes a driving force. Not only are you doing a disservice to yourself but those around you suffer too.

The key to overcoming burnout is to carve out some "you" time in your day. Start by delegating household tasks to other family members. Yes, you may have to settle for less than a perfect home, but so what. The goal is to lessen your burden so that you can rediscover the balance your body needs.

Aim to create a more balanced and happier lifestyle and serenity will follow.

September 15

"The best person for the job is you!"

When you're depressed, it helps to know that there is someone by your side who is caring, compassionate and who understands what you are going through. Guess what? The best person for that job is you!

When you're feeling down, be compassionate and patient with yourself. Treat yourself gently, as you would a good friend. Give yourself time and space to get through the tough times.

Remember, you have survived hard times before; and as you treat yourself with TLC, you will get through this rough patch, too.

September 16

"Motivation to start anything new comes from why you want to start."

You may think you know why you want to start something new, but this time, approach it differently. This new approach could truly make a difference in whether or not you succeed. Start by creating a list of things you want to get out of your new venture. Carry around a note pad and pen for a few days and write down every single benefit you can think of that relates to your new goal.

After starting something new, it may not take long before your determination to succeed goes by the way side. But wait; don't give up so easily! It's not time to give up but time to recharge your motivation.

The desire, inspiration and motivation to stick with anything new comes from reminding yourself why you started in the first place. Remember that note pad? Find a quiet place and read back through your notes. Remind yourself of why and let the reasons sink in. In no time your determination will return and you'll be back on track toward success.

September 17

"Your intuition is your friend for life."

Intuition is the bridge between the known and the unknown. Yet because we cannot see it or measure it on any instrument, we often disregard that inner voice. "Don't drive down that road," "Call Sally today," "Take that finance course," it whispers, but often we disregard it as an aberration of the mind.

But that soft, pervasive voice is your inner self speaking. Learning to listen for it and act on it is one of the greatest gifts you can give yourself. That voice is the speed dial to your own truths. You instinctively know this, but your civilized, educated brain will often redirect the call and put it hold, sometimes to your detriment.

Make a decision today to listen for that inner knowledge and make a pact with yourself to act on it. Trusting your intuition is the hardest step, but once you make friends with your own inner knowing, your own truth, there is no greater friendship.

September 18

"Refuse to accept limitations."

Self-limiting beliefs are based on fears and doubts that hold you back from doing things you want or need to do. These negative thoughts dwell on your lack of ability, limited smarts, inferior looks, or substandard skills and creativity. In other words, they see your potential as a glass half empty.

When you doubt yourself, you give power to these beliefs. The more you repeat those beliefs in your head the more powerful they become.

One of the most important decisions you can make is to challenge those self-limiting beliefs, to refuse to accept them as the truth. Self-limiting beliefs exist only in your mind. The reality is that you have talent, intelligence and the creativity to do great things.

Believe that as truth, and your life will change forever!

September 19

"You have the opportunity and the responsibility to choose the people in your life."

You are a grown woman. You can and should choose the individuals you spend your time with.

It's important to have people in your life that you know will support you in being your best; people who are there to celebrate your highs and support your lows - people who support you in living a life that reflects your values, not the values of others.

Develop quality relationships with others. Forget about being obligated or pressured to spend time with people who don't support you. In the end, such choices will bring the riches of fulfillment as well as a happier life.

September 20

"In the quest to have more, be more, and do more, you may lose yourself."

It seems that each one of us is in a never-ending quest to have more, be more, and do more. Our lives become a blur of activities that we don't necessarily enjoy. As for the things that we do enjoy, the pleasures and pastimes that recharged our souls remain forever on a "to-do" list. In all the hustle and bustle, it is too easy to lose yourself.

Take control! Don't be afraid to ask for help with those mundane, daily tasks. And, most important, don't feel afraid or guilty about saying "No!" when you need time to recharge.

Deep inside, you know what's most important. Always putting yourself second doesn't serve anyone. Now, take out your "to-do" list and start doing! It's the best way to keep in touch with who you really are.

September 21

"Expectations are barometers of success."

As nice as it would be, you don't just wake up one day feeling confident. Lasting confidence is earned, through successes and accomplishments.

We all place expectations on the outcome of our performance. It's important to remember that such expectations ultimately determine whether you consider yourself successful or not.

If you're consistently not meeting your expectations, redefine them. Make sure they are realistic. And, most importantly, make sure they are your own. When you meet your own realistic expectations, when you measure success by your own barometer (not someone else's), you will feel successful and your confidence will rise.

September 22

"Claim your authentic self and live to your fullest potential."

When you find happiness and success within yourself, you are an authentic person. You know who you really are, without reference to the expectations of peers or society.

To live an authentic life, you must free yourself from superficial values. You must think for yourself, decide what is right for you, and get in touch with your own thoughts, needs and desires. Lastly, you must embrace your own values and live what you believe to be true.

Then, and only then, are you authentic. Then and only then, can you live up to your full potential.

September 23

"Begin it now!"

Take a moment to think about something you'd like to achieve, change or improve in your life.

Without criticizing or blaming, ask yourself these questions:

Have my actions matched up to show that I am truly committed to achieving this goal? Am I really serious about achieving it? How much do I want this and why?

To make things happen you have to take action. The German writer Goethe said, "Whatever you can do or dream that you can do, begin it. Boldness has genius, magic and power in it. Begin it now."

Today, embrace boldness and take a step toward achieving a goal that is important to you. When you take action, the universe has a magical way of meeting you halfway.

September 24

"Persistence overcomes resistance."

When you're persistent you find the power to hold on and persevere in spite of anything. You're able to overcome every obstacle and you do all that's necessary to succeed.

Persistence does not mean you will not fail, but it does mean that when you feel defeated you rise above your disappointment and keep trying. Instead of giving up when all seems hopeless, you find a way to keep going. You simply refuse to give up.

Great things come your way when you endure what seems impossible. No, it's not easy, but remember, big achievements require time. Be patient and don't give up.

Sow persistence and reap success!

September 25

"Concentrate on the few, not the many."

You can think of many things that you want to change or achieve. The problem is, when you set out to do too many things at once, nothing gets the full attention it needs - and in the end, very little is accomplished.

To succeed, you need to set priorities. Choose only one or two things that you want to achieve. Concentrate your efforts exclusively on these goals. Very quickly your efficiency will soar and you will see results.

September 26

"I should get that done; I'll do it later."

Sound familiar? It's called procrastination and we all do it, but for some women it's a way of life.

Procrastination makes you feel indecisive and guilty – indecisive because you choose to postpone what must be done and guilty for not doing, now, what you need to do. The more often you procrastinate, the weaker you feel.

If you're in the habit of putting things off, try this. Next time you're faced with a project, take a look at what you want to accomplish. Tune into the reasons for your resistance and then honestly ask yourself, "Is this something I can start, now?" Most of the time the answer is "Yes." So, start!

See yourself as someone who makes solid decisions. When you commit to something honor yourself and stick with it until it's done. You'll empower yourself and the desire to procrastinate will, slowly, disappear.

September 27

"Unleash your creative power."

Many of us do not see ourselves as naturally creative. We fail to recognize and appreciate our innate abilities. That's because we hold limiting concepts of ourselves and what it means to be creative. The thesaurus says that creativity is also originality, inspiration and imagination. That describes you, doesn't it?

Whatever your calling is in life you have the ability to express creativity through it. Whether you want to improve your personal relationships, plant a garden, furnish a home, or cook a gourmet meal - all these avenues offer opportunities for inspired self-expression.

So, see yourself as original, inspired and imaginative. Then, unleash the creativity within and watch your attitude and accomplishments reach new heights you never thought imaginable.

September 28

"Peace of mind comes when you appreciate what you have, instead of focusing on what's missing."

As we grow up, we start to obsess that our families, partners, homes, cars and jobs need fixing. It's true that some tweaking here and there may be in order; but this kind of focus may make you dwell on what is missing in your life. "If only I had . . ." It's this internal dialogue that makes peace of mind elusive.

Only when you feel thankful for something, can you become more fulfilled and peaceful. Accept what you have and where you are with gratitude. Feel thankful and you will feel more peaceful.

September 29

"The person you choose to be with should support your dreams and respect your values."

B eing accepted is a requirement in all relationships. Nobody wants to be with someone who rejects them for what they believe or judges them for certain traits of their personality.

You're entitled to your own decisions, beliefs, goals, etc. When someone truly loves you, they love the whole package you come in. This includes the physical you, the emotional you, and the dreams and values that come along with you.

After all, that's the true beauty of being an individual. And, the one you choose to be with should be grateful.

September 30

"Whom do you work for?"

N o matter what you do or whom you work with, the work you do must be for you.

If you're an employee in a business, think of yourself as a consultant. Start managing your career as you would your own company. When you do, you place much greater value on your time and skills. You take control! And, when you're in the driver's seat, you can't be shaken by the toughest manager, ruffled by office politics, offended by rumors, or frightened by business dips and organizational changes.

No matter what happens, you'll be okay - because you are your own boss!

October

October 1

"Endless possibilities exist for all of us."

New decisions and changes are frightening but they can also be exhilarating!

No matter what pressures you're under, what tough decisions you face, keep in mind that it is possible to turn chaos and turmoil into an exciting beginning.

Look at all the options life has to offer. Ask yourself how those options fit in with your deepest desires. Whether your desires are intellectual, artistic, spiritual, or physical you can make a decision, now, to make them into realities.

Do this and you will soar over boundaries and recognize that your endless possibilities have no limits.

October 2

"Value yourself."

You have the right to be treated well, to value your own intelligence, to create a satisfying life for yourself, and to value your own creativity. You are worthy of happiness, health, success and love. You deserve to have good friends, fulfilling personal relationships, and strong family bonds.

No matter how many difficulties you face in a day, remember to value yourself. You deserve to have a great relationship with you. Because, you are worth it!

October 3

"Maintain your sanity."

Most of us women can't resist the urge to talk on the phone, feed the baby, go through the day's mail, and cook a meal all at the same time. Many women are experts at combining activities and admittedly there is a sense of satisfaction in being able to do many things at once.

Hold on! When you're juggling like this day in and day out you'll end up feeling fragmented, worn down, and fed up. If it goes on too long, resentment will creep in.

Instead of being Superwoman every minute of every day, take time to slow down. A slower pace is essential to keeping your stress levels in check and helping those around you stay balanced.

October 4

"Change your excuses to self-empowering statements."

As soon as challenges arise, many women can think of a million excuses why they can't be overcome. As soon as a woman loses focus on her goals, she can give a million reasons for why she hasn't moved forward.

Take a moment and think back over the last six months. Did you start something new? Did you quit before you were done? What was your excuse?

Instead of focusing energy on negative excuses, try exchanging them for thoughts that inspire and empower. Examples of empowering and self-motivating statements are, "There is no time like the present;" "I will not quit until I'm finished;" "I am just the person to do this job;" "That didn't work, but I have another idea."

Be creative. Make sure to exchange excuses for statements that give you momentum – and in no time, you'll succeed!

October 5

"What are you telling yourself?"

Positive self-talk is not about telling yourself that bad things in your life don't exist or have not happened. It's not about telling yourself life will be easy if you think the right thoughts. Self-talk is about self-awareness and recognizing how your thoughts affect how you feel and ultimately what you accomplish.

Your thoughts are your self-talk. And, they directly affect the way you feel. Since your feelings dictate your actions, it's important to take notice of the chain of thoughts and events in your life.

This newfound awareness holds the key to making the changes you crave come to pass.

October 6

"Change is necessary to live a life with few regrets."

You only live once. And, it doesn't hurt to think of this from time to time. The worst thing would be to look back on your life, wishing you could have been happier or done more.

Don't let that happen! Now is the time to take a good look at your life and make changes so that you have no regrets.

We all know time flies. Days, weeks, months and years slip away. Don't let them pass you by. Make the necessary changes that bring happy, joyful memories, so you can look back with no regrets.

October 7

"Who are you?"

Imagine for a moment that you are the main character in a novel. Ask these questions of that character. What makes her tick? What turns her on? What are her talents? What are her interests? What values guide her life?

The main character in a book evolves and grows. You must do the same. Get to know yourself and you too will evolve and grow.

Start by asking yourself questions about whom you are and what you like to do. Armed with this newfound knowledge, you'll feel confident in asserting yourself in new and more decisive ways.

And, your life will change – for the better!

October 8

"Admit your mistake! It's your most empowering choice."

We all make mistakes. It's a fact of life. What matters is what you do afterwards.

You have a choice. You can let your mistake torment you, embarrass you, and hold you back. Or, you can admit you made a mistake, learn from it, and move on.

Mistakes are lessons in disguise. You can learn something from each and every one. Next time you make a mistake, act quickly and decisively. Take responsibility and look for the lesson. Use the lesson to reach greater success and good fortune in your life.

Learn from your mistakes. Only then can they empower you to greater heights.

October 9

"Spend some time alone every day."

Spending time alone develops the internal friendship that each woman needs to be truly happy.

It's a time when you ask yourself what you would like to change about yourself and your life. It's a time to explore your dreams and fantasies. It's also a time to listen to yourself and make plans.

If your schedule is so busy that you feel you never have time to yourself, then use the time when you are in the shower or during your commute to work.

Make it a priority to devote time to your internal friendship. As this friendship builds so will the trust you have in yourself.

October 10

"Setting meaningful goals takes courage."

Setting a goal can be a huge challenge. Setting goals can even be intimidating, no less following through with one.

When you set goals you are taking responsibility for the outcome. What's easy about that?

Instead of being fearful or intimidated, praise yourself for your willingness to accept the risk. Growth requires you to venture outside your comfort zone. Be willing to take on the unknown and be courageous when you face it.

Set a goal today that challenges your usual way of thinking. As you exercise your courage through goal setting, prosperity will naturally follow.

October 11

"Listen to your inner wisdom."

A dvice from others may share the benefit of experience. But, not trusting your own inner wisdom can hold you back. Even though the intentions of others are good, sometimes their views and words are negative. They may even encourage you to believe that they know your needs better than you.

When you hear advice that makes you doubt your dreams and abilities, stop! Believe in yourself first and see all other viewpoints from that perspective. Your situation can always change for the better and what you want, though ambitious, is possible. Wisdom offered by others may be absolutely right - but it doesn't mean it's right for you.

You know your strengths and capabilities. You know your ability to hold on to an idea and make it work despite the odds. In the end believe in your own wisdom, first, and thank others for theirs.

October 12

"Your life will always be, to a large extent, what you make it."

Y our life is yours. You own it, and what you make of it is purely up to you. Others may support you in your aspirations, but in the end, it's your creation. You are your one and only boss and with that awareness comes a special responsibility.

Once you accept this responsibility and stop waiting around for others to make you happy, you will become unstoppable. There will be no denying you. Your life will change, all because of you.

So, turn on the green light and go!

October 13

"Never apologize for being nervous."

Whether it's a job interview, a speech, or auditioning for a part in a community play, nervous feelings are inevitable. They happen to everyone.

The difference is how each woman deals with her nervous feelings. First, you should accept them as part of public speaking and know you are not alone in your feelings. Second, don't feel the need to apologize for being nervous. When you do, you only draw attention to it. Keep in mind that even if most of the time you see yourself as nervous, your audience doesn't. And, they don't need to know.

Instead, take a deep breath, stand tall, and speak. You are a confident woman with something important to say - nervousness and all.

October 14

"Change your mental environment by curling up with a good book."

Reading a good book is like taking a mini-vacation. Your attention is absorbed and for a while you forget about everyday challenges.

A good book naturally gives you a moment to relax and forget. It takes you away to another land where your imagination has no limits.

Think of a book that you have been meaning to read and pick it up today. It may be a beloved classic, an old favorite, a biography, or something from the bestseller list. Next, pour yourself a cup of your favorite tea, find a comfortable couch, curl up, and let it take you away.

Bon Voyage!

October 15

"Learn to nurture yourself."

Somewhere along the line many women learn to put the needs of others before their own. In many ways this ability is one of our greatest feminine talents; nurturing is a trait that validates us as women and this quality of our nature should surely be treasured and celebrated.

But, why is it that so many of us feel guilty when it comes to nurturing ourselves? We feel selfish. We believe that we're stealing time away from those that need us. Yet the truth is, you need to nurture yourself before you can successfully nurture others. This may sound self-indulgent, but it's not. By taking care of your own needs, you are recognizing and affirming that your own emotional, physical and mental health is just as important as that of others.

The truth is that, at least some of the time, you have to put yourself and your own needs first. If you love and care for yourself, you're far better equipped to love and care for those that need you.

October 16

"It is impossible to listen when you're talking."

The ability to keep quiet is one of the keys to successfully listening, both in daily life and when seeking communication from within.

Unfortunately, inner quiet is unusual for most of us. Even when alone, we talk to ourselves: we hear the sounds of our own thoughts, remember musical melodies, and so on. We become easily distracted by random memories, noises and other intrusions.

When you learn to listen, it becomes easier to relax. Your mind clears more quickly and attentiveness to your environment is enhanced. As you allow yourself to listen, thoughts become less random and more controllable – and most important, you hear plainly what's going on inside.

October 17

"Energy and passion are contagious."

One of the easiest ways for you to increase your energy and passion is to surround yourself with friends that are energetic and passionate. When you're around women and men that are positive and upbeat, it helps you to feel and act the same way.

Think about it! Which friends leave you feeling better and more enthusiastic about yourself? They are the ones with qualities that make you feel good inside. This is the kind of friend you want to create close relationships with - to spend more time with. As you share time, their traits rub off on you. It won't take long before you are the energetic, joyful and passionate one!

October 18

"In the long run, it's your personal relationships that really matter."

With today's busy lifestyles, it's all too easy to put relationships on the backburner and take them for granted. Even though you may have every intention of spending regular time with your partner, hectic schedules get in the way and you end up running in every direction except toward each other.

Yet, you know that your personal relationships are paramount to personal fulfillment. Be sure to set some time aside each week to rediscover the people that mean most to you. Be alone with that person, talk, enjoy your time together, and renew your relationship.

After all, in this life, your loved ones are what really matter.

October 19

"Anything that you should have done, but didn't, ties you to your past."

Is your mental and emotional clutter getting in the way of a fulfilling life? It's time to clean out the "need-to's," "have-to's," and "ought-to's," from your past. When you have regrets it's tough to move forward and grow.

Put the past in the past. Return anything you borrowed. Make apologies where needed. Get your bills up to date. Send the card or gift you forgot to send. Make the phone call you need to make.

Taking care of these things cleans your mental slate and eliminates any regrets or resentments you may harbor.

Now, take a deep breath; look ahead. Both your conscience, and your future vision, is clear.

October 20

"When you try something new, you have little to lose and much to gain."

Of course success is never guaranteed, but that does not mean you should not try. Take comfort in knowing that even if you fail you are still gaining life experiences and making deposits into your bank of wisdom. You really have lost nothing in your pursuit. You have come out smarter, wiser and more prepared for your next challenge.

Arise to your next challenge. If you find yourself thinking, "What if I fail?" try turning that question around. Instead, ask yourself, "What if I succeed?" That's how winners think!

October 21

"Work is a reward, not a punishment."

If you enjoy your work, you also enjoy what comes with it, such as peace of mind, enjoyment and fulfillment. If you don't enjoy your work, then days are tedious and each one drags by.

The truth is, you'll never achieve pure happiness unless you like what you do. Your fulfillment is in direct proportion to the amount of pleasure you derive from daily tasks.

If you truly despise your job, stop punishing yourself and do something about it. The rewards you feel from doing what you want to do are priceless. You only live once and there is no reason I can think of not to enjoy it!

October 22

"Your appointment is confirmed."

You set appointments all the time, with doctors, dentists, accountants, contractors and hair salons. More often than not the appointments you set actually take place. Once in a while you have to cancel an appointment, but that's okay, because you reschedule it and place the new date and time on your calendar.

There's one person, though, that you might never think to set an appointment with. That person is you!

Why not schedule an appointment with yourself and write it on your calendar? Schedule some time to do something fun with yourself. Make it a definite date.

When the time comes, keep the appointment, just as you would any other. After a few appointments with the all-important you, you'll wonder why you didn't do it sooner.

October 23

*"Making personal changes takes courage, planning,
persistence and will."*

Questions like "What do I want to accomplish?" and "What
will make me happiest?" are difficult to answer. What's
even more difficult is cultivating a plan to achieve them. But, you
must. Making a plan gives you direction and purpose.

Take some time to decide what really matters. Brainstorm and
figure out what you need to do to make things happen. No one
but you can do this. If you don't, you risk letting others make
plans for you.

Don't settle for less than you are worth. Create and cultivate
your goals and aspirations. Think about them, decide how you are
going to achieve them, and patiently pursue them.

It's all up to you and you can do it! Take action today.

October 24

"You are already perfect."

When you were born you were perfect. You were naturally
assertive. You knew exactly what you wanted and what
you didn't want. Instinctively you knew what gave you joy and
what made you unhappy. You were an amazing and awesome
being. You possessed potential to be anything and anybody. Yet
somewhere along in your life's journey you may have lost touch
with that perfection.

We are all molded by our parents, by our friends, and by
society to be the person we are today. On top of that each one of
us has had our share of problems and sadness, too. Yet there is
one thing that hasn't changed. We are still the same perfect being
that we always were.

Despite where life may have taken you, you are still perfect.
You don't need to look outside yourself; you need to reconnect
with your own perfection.

Today, take time to experience the exquisite beauty of your own unique self.

October 25

"Take care in what you say."

A smile that is insincere can be a turn off. Saying, "Have a nice day," without meaning it, does not go unnoticed. The person who was hurt or deceived probably won't accept an apology with little depth.

We all have feelings. Nobody is unique. How your feelings affect what you say should not go unnoticed. It's okay to be frustrated or mad. And, it's perfectly normal and acceptable to express emotions. Just remember, when you do, be aware of how your frank expressions or your true feelings may make someone else feel.

Such awareness brings sincerity to your smiles and meaning to your greetings.

October 26

"Allowing dreams to emerge, gives you the strength to make them real."

If you allow yourself to dream, to aspire, you can't help but to begin to plan.

Once you have a plan, you can begin taking steps to make your dreams real. Whether you've always wanted to heal the planet or just have more time to yourself, today is the time to do it. Now is the time to take advantage of your energy, wisdom, enthusiasm and vitality.

Make your dreams important in your life. Let them come to the surface and take on meaning. Once you do, you will feel better about yourself. And, the enthusiasm and energy to pursue your dreams will soar!

October 27

"Give yourself permission to say, 'No.'"

As young girls, many of us were taught to always try to please people. We were told it was important to be seen as nice and non-confrontational. As a result, we went out of our way to do things that people wanted. We became people pleasers, afraid to rock the boat.

Is this still your mantra?

Recognize and appreciate that you have a right to do what's right for you. There is no need to always feel obligated to please others, at your expense.

If a friend asks you do something when you have other priorities, say "No." If the school asks you to volunteer when you'd rather enjoy lunch with friends, say "No."

Don't feel obligated to offer an excuse. Give yourself permission to say, "No!" Because a balanced life includes pleasing yourself, as well as others.

October 28

"Life works best with fewer non-negotiables."

Non-negotiables are stances you take where you're not willing to budge an inch. You probably have non-negotiables with your partner, kids, parents and your job. They can be things that you want, things that you don't want, or your opinions and points of view.

Only you can decide where to draw the line. There are certainly things in your life that, no matter what, are non-negotiable. End of discussion! But if your list of non-negotiables is long then you may be making life more difficult than necessary.

Challenge your non-negotiables. Are they all really set in stone? Remember, sometimes you need to be willing to give a little to receive greater harmony and good will.

October 29

"Make self-talk positive and self-empowering."

Keeping self-talk in line with what you want to achieve is just a thought away. Listen to your thoughts. Recognize your inner dialogue. When self-talk limits you, question it, challenge it, and change it.

For instance, if you hear yourself thinking, "Here I go again, making a stupid mistake. I'll never get it right," question your inner thoughts. Ask, "Why am I talking to myself so negatively?" Then, challenge this negative dialogue by telling yourself, "I can get things right."

You can change your inner voice. Just think, "That was no big deal. I'll fix it, right now." Then, fix it. It's nearly impossible to ignore your internal dialogue. Since you can't ignore it, acknowledge it. But, don't let it discourage you. When it's negative, turn it around. Tell yourself something positive and self-empowering. With this kind of positive self-talk, you can achieve anything!

October 30

"It's not what happens to you, but how you react, that matters."

There are two parts to every woman's world, the inner world and the outer world. The inner world is you - the outer world is where things happen to you.

You have complete control over your inner world. You choose everything you believe, say or do. Your outer world is different. Things happen that you cannot control, like death, disaster and natural forces.

Just remember it's how you react to the events in your outer world that affects you. Use the strength and power of your inner world to control your reactions and it will make all the difference in your life.

October 31

"Finish what you begin."

When you make a heart-felt decision to finish something meaningful and then do it, something amazing happens. You feel energized and all the worry and fear that you felt in the beginning miraculously disappears.

Your mind is free! You no longer feel guilty. The burden is gone and you don't beat yourself up for avoiding what needed to be done.

In the end, when you finish what you begin, you're naturally motivated to do more. So, if you feel like quitting, keep in mind that wonderful feelings are waiting at the end of every meaningful task.

Just for you!

November

November 1

"To have compassion for others, you must first have compassion for yourself."

Self-compassion is the ability to acknowledge your shortcomings, your vulnerability and your humanness - yet still perceive yourself as the lovable woman that you are.

You can never truly give to another if you feel empty inside. You can force yourself to give, but your giving won't be genuine and you will feel resentful. This is why it's so important to care for yourself first.

No one can give a gift they don't already possess.

So, practice self-compassion today. Meet your own deepest needs. Take time for yourself, by listening to your inner voice and feeling your own emotions. Know that they are okay, because you are a woman and you are human.

November 2

"Nothing enriches your life like a friendship."

You know what it's like when you get together with a close friend whom you haven't seen for a long time? It's like you've never been apart; you just pick up where you left off.

Your connection with your friend goes back to all your shared experiences, values and feelings. Time does not diminish those in any way. Your connection endures time and remains strong.

Think of a friend that is dear to you and that you haven't connected with lately. Pick up the phone and give her a call. It will make your whole day - and brighten hers, too.

November 3

"Goals that you believe in are the ones that really count."

Does the effort you put into achieving your goals feel more like a burden, than a welcome challenge? This is a sign that your goals are not your own.

You may be trying to live up to the ideals of your spouse, friends or parents. You may even be trying to live up to society's version of success and perfection.

Goals set for you by others may not be realistic. And, the more you strive for goals that are far from your heart, the greater your dissatisfaction and frustration may become.

For you to feel happy inside and out, you must pursue what is important to you.

Never think that what you want is not good enough. It is! As you set and achieve goals that really matter, you will feel more successful, positive and optimistic.

November 4

"Your life is a series of experiences."

Each life experience makes you stronger, more knowledgeable and more prepared for what lies ahead.

Though it may not seem like it at the time, the setbacks and hardships you face actually help you march forward.

Don't isolate yourself from life experiences. They instruct you and guide you into your future. Learn from your experiences. They are the best teacher anyone could ask for.

November 5

"What you think about most molds your attitude."

Your thoughts and beliefs are a mold for your attitude. If your thoughts are negative and self-defeating, your attitude will be the same. If your thoughts are positive and uplifting, your outlook will be the same.

What you think about most makes you what you are. It's the repetition of the same old negative thoughts that keeps you stuck. If you want to change your attitude, use the same repetitive method. Repetitive, self-empowering thoughts are the key.

This transformation will be gradual and require persistence. Once you adopt these positive affirmations, don't get discouraged if your negative thoughts don't immediately disappear. Keep at it and you will soon see definite results.

If you can change your attitude, you can change your life!

November 6

"When waiting is the hardest choice."

A re you facing a difficult time in your life?
Give yourself the gift of patience. Patience is the main ingredient necessary to get through difficult times.

Yes, it's hard to be patient! But, without patience, you would have no hope. And, if the universe was organized so that your desires materialized instantly, that wouldn't serve you either.

Patience helps you grow. It nourishes both compassion and empathy. So, embrace patience. Ultimately this makes you a stronger woman.

Be patient!

November 7

"Waiting gives you time for thought."

T ry something different today. If you happen to be standing in line and it's moving slowly, instead of becoming agitated by the wait, focus on the positive side.

You now have a few extra minutes to review your errands and make sure you have not forgotten anything; a few extra minutes to think about a project at work; a few extra minutes to chuckle about something funny your child said earlier in the day.

Don't tie up your emotional energy or become agitated or anxious about situations you can't control. Instead, go with the flow. This change of attitude will make a huge difference in your day.

November 8

"A sure fire way to obtain happiness is to bring happiness to someone else."

Most of us don't really give much thought to happiness. We just know whether we feel happy or not. If you're not happy, you may go searching for it. You may think happiness will come with material things or relationships. Often it doesn't.

If you feel that people react negatively or offensively to things that you do and say, it may be that you share your troubles with others too often. After a while people begin to avoid you and that makes unhappiness worse.

Lasting happiness comes from sharing your positive attitude with others. The more you share the more you will get it in return. Happiness also comes from serving others, like finding little ways to make others happy.

Remember that you have the power to attract anything in your life. Try happiness.

November 9

"Breaking out of limiting beliefs is like opening a door to another world."

Beliefs are a set of generalizations you make about yourself, others and your life. They form your version of reality, based on what you feel and perceive about your experiences.

Beliefs help you set rules by which to conduct your life. Guess what? Beliefs are not facts, even though we act on them as if they were facts.

If you believe you are not a good athlete, you're probably a bad one. If you believe you are horrible at math, then you're destined to fail your next test. Remember, beliefs either free us or limit us.

When we break past limiting beliefs, we enter a whole new world.

So, believe you CAN do it. And ... you probably will!

November 10

"If you have unresolved family conflicts, lay them to rest."

When it comes to family, we all tend to carry unpleasant memories with us throughout our lives. If this goes unchanged we can become bitter and resentful.

If you have deep family issues that are hard to forgive and forget, make today the day you move forward. Put them behind you and try to be more positive about the time you have now. You cannot change the bad things that have happened to you, but you can choose to stop letting them control you.

Life is too short to carry grudges that separate you from those people that you want near and dear to your heart.

November 11

"What kind of old age are you planning?"

Unfortunately, there is no guarantee that your future will be bright and cheerful. You have probably seen women that shut themselves away from the world, as they get older. Too often, these women fade into an aimless, sad and lonely existence.

You may have also seen vibrant older women, who grew into self-assured, active and happy women, with purpose and energy. Plan now for your future, it will be here sooner than you think. Remember that vibrant women grow into a vibrant maturity.

November 12

"Speak up, it will do your self-confidence wonders."

If you're in a meeting at work or at a family gathering don't be afraid to share your thoughts, opinions and ideas. They're just as important as the thoughts, opinions and ideas of the others in the room.

When you don't share your thoughts because you fear how they will be received and the reaction they may trigger, you slowly chip away at your self-confidence.

If the thought of speaking up makes your whole body tense, then start with smaller one on one conversations. This is perfect practice for the important occasions that will surely follow.

November 13

"Try physical, mental and emotional ways to lighten the burden of stress."

Stress is a fact of life. Every one of us encounters it.

If your work is stressful, if you're a single parent or a caretaker of an elderly parent, or if you're grieving for someone you love, your stress level has probably peaked.

Since it's impossible to avoid stress, we must deal with it. The key in dealing with stress it learning how to de-stress. It's all about opening your valve and releasing the pressure.

Music, walking, laughing, meditating, curling up with a good book and massages are all great ways to bring calm back in to your life - even if it is just for a moment. Don't forget to take care of yourself, it is only when you do that the stresses of your life seem easier to handle.

November 14

"Motivation comes from action."

Motivation comes from doing, moving and taking action!

The real excitement begins when you start something and see it begin to take shape. Once you experience success as a direct result of your efforts and enthusiasm, your motivation will rise and carry you through.

If you are waiting to feel motivated, just do something. Just start! Make your motto, "No more waiting - just doing!" That is the secret to the momentum of motivation.

November 15

"You were born with the capacity to believe."

You were born with a capacity for great courage, for trust in your surroundings, and for faith in yourself. But something may have happened along the way that changed this positive capacity.

If you were criticized at an early age and denied encouragement by those you trusted. Slowly but surely you came to believe that something was wrong with you. Over time, such beliefs may appear as the absolute truth – a definition of your identity.

Guess what? It's simply not true! You are perfect and it's time to act that way. As hard as it may be to regain your self-esteem, you can forget and forgive what happened when you were young. You can regain the courage, trust and faith that are your birthright, by recognizing that, although youthful disillusionment can't be changed, it can be overcome.

November 16

"Count your blessings."

Perhaps one of the simplest ways to change your mood or mental outlook is to remind yourself of all the good things in your life. Reflecting on how far you have come, what you have already accomplished, and what you have learned, can be very encouraging.

Appreciating your dearest friends, your closest family members, your favorite possessions, and of course yourself can bring a smile to your face.

If you need a lift or an attitude adjustment, try to appreciate and reflect on the good things. Count your blessings. It can be done anytime and any place.

November 17

"Dare to dance outside the lines."

Today is the day to give yourself permission to break the rules, to move outside the boundaries of your usual way of looking at things. For the time being, forget about practical, realistic ideas. Dare to go beyond the self-censorship that comes from worrying about what other people think.

When you follow your heart and dismiss unimportant "shoulds," you open the door to creative, spiritual and personal breakthroughs. Try it - today!

November 18

"Your intuition is a guiding light."

Your intuition is your quiet inner voice. It helps you make decisions, gives you direction and acts as your guide.

Intuition talks to you in different ways. Sometimes it's a strong feeling or an inner "knowing." Sometimes it's a sudden flash of inspiration or a moment of clarity. No matter how intuition speaks to you, know it always wants the best for you.

Next time you're faced with an important decision, calm your mind, let go of self-serving emotions or thoughts and let your intuition speak. At first, it may be subtle. But, with awareness and practice, you can recognize it instantly.

Trust your intuition to be your guiding light. It will never disappoint you!

November 19

"Accepting yourself as you are takes courage."

Who are you? Do you know? Take time to think about your values and goals. What do you believe in? What is important to you?

Decide that you will never compromise your integrity by trying to be or say or feel something that is not true for you. Have the courage to accept yourself as you really are, not as an ideal or as someone else thinks you should be.

Most of all, know that at the end of the day, you are wonderful woman capable of wonderful things.

November 20

"You can't always control your circumstances."

Your life can change at any time, from harmonious to difficult. The reality is that you have no control over circumstances that may turn your life upside down.

But there is something you can control. That something is your reaction to the situation. When you accept this and resist the urge to blame and act as the victim, you regain control.

Be mindful when life gets tough. Never give away what power you do possess, when confronted with a bad situation.

Be calm. Be strong. You can do it!

November 21

"Finding answers isn't everything."

We don't always know why things happen. Disappointments and difficulties may never be explained. For example, you may never fully understand why management passed you up for a promotion or why a partner left you for someone else. No doubt there will be times in your life when you are left scratching your head trying to figure out, "Why?"

Letting go when there is no understanding that "Why?" is very hard. Our culture places such emphasis on finding answers. But, finding answers isn't everything. Your life should not stop when you don't understand events. Instead, you must learn to let go.

So, get on with your life. Regain your energy and passion. Let go of the frustration of asking "Why?" and you clear the deck for a brighter future!

November 22

"Don't let a small argument ruin a great friendship."

Arguments are much more than two points of view that don't coincide. It's inevitable that disagreements will occasionally occur between people who are close. What's more, occasional arguments can be a healthy indication of two confident personalities who feel comfortable enough to express their true feelings.

Next time you argue with a friend, accept that you have different points of view – and get over it! Your friendship is far more important than anything you may quarrel over. Don't sacrifice the relationship you've built together for the sake of winning a point.

If apologies are needed, make them. If forgiveness is required, offer it. By moving past the argument, you both come out winners and stay friends!

November 23

"Never underestimate yourself."

Many people put themselves down, by pointing out their inabilities, inadequacies and weaknesses. They underestimate their capabilities, competence and potential. Unfortunately, this is especially true for women.

Does this ring true with you? Take a closer look at yourself and tune into what you say and do. Vow to never, ever underestimate yourself or limit what you can achieve. You are a woman with huge amounts of talent and skill, screaming to be seen and heard!

Instead of thinking in terms of what you "can't" do, think in terms of what you "can" do. This will let your talents shine!

Remember, you have the ability. You're perfectly adequate. You possess limitless potential, because you're you!

November 24

"Lighten up the serious side of life."

When you take time to play, you connect with your childlike self. Fun connects you with that spontaneous part of you that makes life enjoyable.

To have fun you don't need to spend a lot of money. You don't need to do something extreme or be around witty people. You can have fun doing something simple, with yourself.

Try turning up the radio in your car and singing out loud. Who cares if someone is watching you? You'll probably never see them again. And, if you do, won't it be great to know you're having more fun than they are?

Take some time today to reconnect with the fun side of yourself. It liberates your joy when you do!

November 25

"Success is a meaningful lifestyle, not just a business."

How many people do you know that have aggressively achieved their dreams yet they never feel complete? What happened?

They have sacrificed their health, relationships and personal needs for success, without knowing what's most important to them.

There's a lesson here for every one of us. Before you can be truly successful, your core values and beliefs must be aligned with your efforts. In other words, your heart must lead your labors. Without this, true fulfillment will never come your way.

November 26

"Remember when you were first in love?"

Remember the small things you did to show your love to your boyfriend? Things like a phone call in the middle of the day just to talk or say "I love you," a love note left in his car, a foot massage, simple gifts, and cooking romantic dinners. Remember those days?

As time passes you get weighted down with simply living life and forget all those things that made the difference in the beginning.

Rekindle and reconnect with your relationship by consciously going back and doing the things that you did when your love first began to grow. Who knows? You may fall in love all over again!

November 27

"If your life is a campaign against things, the things you fight will expand."

Is there is something in your life that you don't want? If so, then stop worrying about it and stop talking about it. You may not realize it, but the energy you put into fighting the issue, keeps it alive. Whenever you agonize over something, you breathe life into it.

Happily, the reverse is also true. Withdraw your energy and focus and the issue shrinks, until it goes away. It's time to give yourself the relief you deserve.

Decide to truly let go of what you are fighting, emotionally, and watch as it evaporates and no longer robs your spirit.

November 28

"Bye-Bye Critic!"

Wouldn't it be great if you could just turn off your negative self-talk once and for all? You would be so much happier. The truth is you can't. But, you can control it. It is so important that you do this before negative self-talk depletes your self-esteem.

When you're constantly telling yourself things like, "I'm not good at anything," "I can't get that job," or "I'll never lose weight," it doesn't take long before you start to believe it. And, when you believe it, you act in ways to support it.

Remember that all women have negative thoughts. Women with high self-esteem are the ones that have exchanged negative self-talk for positive inner dialogue. They successfully tune out the negative chatter and replace it with an "I can" and "I will" attitude.

Guess what? So can you.

November 29

"Each new day is a building block for reaching your goals and dreams."

Personal goals and dreams are not formed over night; they are built with each passing day. It's important that you do something each day toward fulfilling your personal dreams. Every effort, no matter how small or insignificant, can make a difference.

All those daily "blocks" build on one another and slowly but surely, add up. Be patient with yourself and never give up. Your tower will slowly grow and sooner than you think, you'll be standing at the top!

November 30

"Relax and enjoy life's journey."

Every day you're bombarded with an ever-increasing number of opportunities, yet you don't seem to have enough time to get things done. If that isn't enough, you believe you're not working quickly enough to keep up with the nonstop flow of information streaming out of your computer. Worse yet, you feel as if you'll be left in the dust if you don't keep up.

The truth is, there will never be enough time to get everything done, so, don't kill yourself trying.

You can face overwhelming challenges, yet still make each day purposeful by keeping in mind a clear intention of what you want to do. Resolve to stay focused on accomplishing important tasks. Be willing to say "No" when you are asked to add responsibilities that are not in harmony with your aspirations.

Life is not meant to be a struggle but a balanced and joyful journey.

December

December 1

"Your hunch is trying to tell you something."

How many times have you said to yourself, "I knew I should have done that" or "Why didn't I listen to myself?" Your intuition was talking to you, and you ignored it. Often your intuition gets dismissed because it tells you something that doesn't fit with your logical or habitual way of thinking.

Trust yourself. Your intuition is very powerful. It will lead you down the best possible path for you, if you let it. The next time you have a hunch about a certain idea to pursue, a decision to make, or a person to contact, do it.

When you trust your intuition, you live with no regrets.

December 2

"Perceptions are just that, perceptions."

Your perceptions of the way things are reflect the way you were raised, your experiences, and the successes or failures you've had in life. It's tough, but everyone must recognize that things are what they are, regardless of perceptions. In other words, accepting things as they are and not as you wish them to be, makes getting through tough times easier.

So, be open to adjusting your perceptions. Check-in with yourself to see if these perspectives are working for you. As you do, you gain greater inner control and this smoothes out the rocky road of life!

December 3

"What are your patterns of criticism?"

Is there repetitive critical feedback that you receive on a regular basis? If so, this feedback is worthy of your attention. Repeated criticisms are opportunities to learn about yourself. Perhaps over the years, you have been told you're an "ice queen," you're unapproachable, or you're shy. Though these criticisms may not be true or may reflect another's misinterpretations, they still deserve your attention.

So, stop being defensive. Instead of resisting, examine the feedback. Perhaps your shyness is coming across to others as aloofness, arrogance or hardheartedness. Though the truth may be the exact opposite, recognize that such impressions may close wonderful doors of opportunity.

If negative feedback repeats itself, give it thoughtful attention. A little attention now may open many big doors, later.

December 4

"A chip off the old block."

In our youth, we didn't appreciate being called a "chip off the old block." But, this was really a compliment to our inner powers.

Deep within you is a rock of strength, an immovable foundation of physical, emotional, mental and spiritual muscle. You empower yourself when you take charge of that inner muscle, for this is your real self, your true character.

Each of us is a combination of the physical self, the emotional self, the mental self, and the spiritual self. When you nurture these "selves," you naturally grow more creative, energetic and empowered to enjoy life.

So, don't be afraid of becoming a "chip off the old block." For within you, at this moment, is a firm foundation that will always remain unshakeable.

December 5

"Confident women focus on controllables."

Contrary to what most people think, confident women sometimes doubt themselves and their abilities. So, being confident doesn't necessarily mean that you will never have self-defeating thoughts or feelings. You will. Doubt, concern and nervousness are real feelings and they happen whether you're confident or not.

Instead of spending time doubting themselves or worrying about what they cannot do or might not be able to do, confident women focus on what they can control. They turn their concentration away from uncertainty and toward conviction.

You can do the same. When you concentrate on the "cans" and forget the "can'ts," your self-confidence soars.

December 6

"You're entitled to a life."

W hen was the last time you slowed down enough to consider your own needs? With so many things to do and so many places to be, you probably haven't thought about yourself lately.

Taking care of your self does great things for you. It makes you less irritable, less anxious, and more satisfied. With consistent self-care you feel energized, centered, strong and willing. You feel like you are in the driver's seat of your life, which is precisely where you belong.

When you find yourself jumping to the demands of others, slow down and remember that you are entitled to a life, too, and it's perfectly okay to say, "No."

December 7

"Results will take as long as they take."

I t is so easy to give up if you don't see expected results, immediately. This is especially true with exercise. You drag yourself to the gym and you sweat and burn. The pounds you planned to lose in three weeks remain stubbornly in place. Discouragement sets in and you want to give up.

Don't worry! This is a common experience for everyone. The good news is that you can turn things around. The secret to not giving up is to practice mindful exercise. Instead of counting your chickens before they hatch, enjoy each moment of your workout for its own sake. Experience exercise as an enjoyable healthy escape from the real world.

While exercising, your mind may stray from your movements. But, stay mindful with each movement. Exist in the moment and gently remind yourself to focus. As you stay focused, without demanding rewards, the exercise itself becomes its own reward – and you will see the results you expect.

December 8

"Things that cause low spirits may stay by your side if you let them."

If you've been feeling depressed, discouraged or bummed out for a while, you may just be making a comfortable bed for your unhappy feelings. Who wants to leave a comfortable bed? Not me!

Low spirits are kept alive and well when you rehearse depressing thoughts in your mind over and over again. Guess what? It's time for you to make an intelligent decision, and that decision is for change.

Start thinking in terms of possibilities and opportunities instead of things that bring you down. It's hard at first and you may have to force yourself, but with a little practice, your spirits will improve and the blue funk will subside.

December 9

"Do you treat your friends better than you treat yourself?"

Being a good friend to yourself is not selfish. It's essential. Take any situation and ask, "What would I do for a friend if she were in my shoes?" Would you do the same for yourself?

When you compare how you treat yourself to how you treat your friends, it's easy to see how to be your own friend. Your happiness is based on how good a friend you are to yourself. Both your self-esteem and self-confidence rely on it.

Not only are you happier when you can trust yourself to be your friend, but it becomes easier to be a good friend to others and recognize when others are good friends to you.

December 10

"Stop fearing the unknown and move forward."

Do these sound familiar? "I'm too old to do something new." "I won't be any good at it." "People will laugh." Are these the kinds of things you tell yourself when opportunity strikes?

When you determine the result or the outcome before you even start, you have already considered rejection or failure. And, when this happens, it's easy to come up with excuses for not even trying.

The secret is to disconnect the outcome from the process. This is when you release the fear and give yourself the opportunity for success.

Think about it, you cannot possibly know the outcome before you try. Nobody can! So, trust yourself and get out there and do it.

December 11

"Measures of success are integral to realizing your aspirations."

When you set goals, it's important to make them measurable so you can keep score of your small and large successes along the way.

The very act of setting a goal and breaking it down into smaller parts and then completing those parts, one-by-one, will make you feel accomplished.

Remember that you can't hit a target you can't see!

Identify and clarify the smaller parts. With each smaller goal achieved, reward yourself because you're now one step closer to your dreams – something to celebrate and be proud of.

December 12

"Satisfaction is sweet when you succeed in spite of discouraging words."

Do you have someone in your life that's knocking down your dreams? Someone who's trying to make you quit? If so, do the opposite of what they are saying. Let their discouraging words motivate you to succeed.

Yes, it's hard at first, especially if you've been listening to and giving in to those who say you can't do it. Decide, right now, not to listen anymore. Try your hardest to block out the discouragement and forge ahead.

Just imagine how good you will feel when you accomplish what you want to do. There is no sweeter success than reaching a goal when others told you, "No!"

December 13

"Jealousy is an emotion we can live without."

When you are jealous of someone else, your positive attitude suffers.

When tempted to compare yourself to a woman who is more beautiful or successful than most, you have a choice. You can choose to admire her fine attributes or let the green-eyed monster have its way. If you choose jealousy, you will become negative, learn to doubt yourself and cultivate both fear and anger. But, when you choose admiration, you nurture an inner awe and wonder, which is too often lost as children grow into adults.

Turn jealousy into admiration. Stop comparing yourself to those with wonderful qualities. Replace negative feelings with appreciation and admiration, and appreciation of your own great qualities will grow!

December 14

"Gratitude does wonders for your attitude."

Gratitude is one of those words that you don't hear very often, but it is one that can do magic when it comes to shifting your attitude. Make a list of the things that you are most thankful for and make it a comprehensive list. This list holds your most cherished times, possessions and people in your life.

When you're having one of those bad days and you need to feel better, more positive and more resourceful, refer back your Gratitude List.

After all, what you are most grateful for matters most.

December 15

"A woman without special gifts,
just an I won't quit! attitude, will succeed."

Everyone wants to be a success in life. But, unless you make a commitment to never quit no matter what, it may never happen.

The one thing that makes a woman successful is persistence. It's not talent, not ability, nor education. Just plain old persistence!

Life will always present you with opportunities to succeed, as well as reasons to quit. Rise above the temptation to quit and find an incentive not to give in.

Today, make an 'I'll never quit!' commitment to yourself. Because you can do anything if you try.

December 16

"Resilience is the key to survival."

If you and your partner have a history of power struggles, nasty arguments and broken trust, you have little to draw on when times are hard.

On the other hand, if you and your partner have a history of trust, partnership, respect, friendship and kindness, you have built up enough resilience and strength to endure the bad times. Vital relationships fill our days with humor, caring and good conversation.

Now is a great time to look at your relationships. Do you have a cushion of resilience to fall back on? If not, it's never too late to start building one.

December 17

"C'mon! Give it a shot."

The fear of not knowing how something will turn out is enough to make anyone say, "Forget it." Rather than dealing with problems head on, sometimes it's easier to ignore them and hope they'll go away. When we're tired of trying, it's tempting to think that, since nothing has worked in the past, we're powerless.

Does any of this ring a bell? If so, it's probably because you put way too much pressure on yourself to have things always work out well. With a mindset like this you're missing out on opportunities, relief and good fortune, simply because you didn't try.

There are no guarantees in any of our lives. Things may or may not work out. Just because they "may not" work out, it's not an excuse not to try.

Next time you find yourself saying, "Forget it," or "No thanks," give it a shot and say "Why not?" instead. Jump in with both feet and see what happens!

December 18

"Beauty is only skin-deep."

Your skin is a mirror; it reflects whatever is going on inside your body and mind. Sure, you can always cover your skin with concealers and makeup. But without physical nourishment and spiritual self-care, a woman can rarely be truly beautiful.

If you're feeling run down and at your wits end, look in the mirror. Your skin will show it. If you're living an unhealthy life style and not getting enough rest, look again. Your lifestyle leaves its fingerprint on your skin.

Remember, the most beautiful you is on the inside, but the most visible you is on the outside. The stronger your spirit, the more beautiful your body. That's why, beauty is only skin-deep!

December 19

"Your life is much more than meets the eye."

When you feel stressed out, burned out and maxed out, it's natural to conclude that life is hard. Wait a minute! Take a step back and reflect. Think of all the things that you are thankful for. You have your health, your family, and all those little things you normally take for granted.

When it seems that you're rough-riding the coattails of life, watch a sunset, listen to good music, or delve into an engrossing book. Allow yourself time to reflect on the gifts you have been given, both big and small.

Sometimes we need to step back, to look clearly at who we are and what we have. Life is always made up of more than meets the eye. Once we see this, we can put things back in perspective and regain a sense of serenity.

December 20

"Life is what you make it."

No one is responsible for your happiness, sadness or success. No one but you. Yes, you!

The day you take complete responsibility for yourself and your choices is the day you start a journey toward grand personal fulfillment.

You're the only one that lives your life. Believe it or not, you do have the power to succeed at anything you choose. The strength to fulfill your dreams is within you, at this very moment. Accepting responsibility without excuses, frees your power to achieve.

You can do it. So, do it today!

December 21

"Doubts, a way to learn, not a way of life."

Millions of people have doubts every day. Nobody is immune. Instead of holding onto nagging doubts forever, use hesitations in a positive way. Employ doubts to propel you forward.

When faced with doubt, ask yourself, "Why do I have this feeling?" See it as a sign that something needs your attention. Take a moment for constructive thought.

As you look for the answer to what is causing your doubts, you may discover truths disguised by the hustle and bustle of life. Don't stop until the reason for your doubt is clear. After you discover it, you can take action. Only then can you can let go of doubt - and doubt can let go of you!

December 22

"A small change in your mindset
may make all the difference in the world."

Certain attitudes and beliefs mold a positive self-image. When you have a positive mindset, you know perfection is not a requirement for success, that it's better to deal with problems than ignore them, that setting your own standards is healthier than comparing yourself with others, and especially, that self-forgiveness should be exercised daily.

You may not realize the potency of these attitudes and beliefs. But, beliefs and attitudes are the tools that make achieving goals possible. They also protect you from stress and boost your self-esteem.

So, reflect on your beliefs. Zero in on the ones that are slowing you down. Remember, small changes of mind can lead to big rewards that make all the difference in the world!

December 23

"A vote of confidence."

Are you someone who quietly sets out to reach her goals or are you someone who tells the world exactly what you're up to, loud and clear?

Either way, it's great. You're focusing on a new life ahead. But if you do tend toward being the quieter type, why not take some time today to tell at least one person how proud you are of yourself for making this commitment to reach a valued goal?

There's got to be one person with whom you could share your journey. A coworker? A neighbor? A friend?

So speak up. Tell someone about it. Make your effort even more real by hearing yourself talk about it out loud. It will solidify your commitment that much more and could just be the vote of confidence you need!

December 24

"Letting the world know the real you,
is instrumental to your growth."

Have you ever noticed how children love to dress up? They love the thrill of pretending to be a princess or a butterfly. What about you? Do you still play make-believe? Do people see you for whom you are or do they see someone different?

Often, we make the choice to hide ourselves, allowing only a select few (family or friends) to see the "real" us. With everyone else, we put on a mask so they see what we want them to see (especially if our self-confidence is low). They may see a happy face that actually hides a ton of pain or insecurities.

I want you to be your best. A good place to start is to acknowledge and embrace the real you, and proudly display it to the world.

Yes, for many that's hard because we don't want to get hurt, it's just easier to put up a front. But living this way, you bury the woman you've always wanted to be. You owe it to yourself, your friends, and your family to not keep yourself under wraps. Today, ditch your old self-imposed costume for a new, better version...the real you!

December 25

"Perfectionism is a state of mind."

There will be times when you fall back into your old negative patterns. It happens. When it does, most likely you'll feel completely furious with yourself and consider giving up. But wait! Before you do anything drastic - think about it first.

Believing that if you can't do something completely right, you may as well not do it at all, is at the heart of perfectionism. And this is something that's derailed countless women trying to make changes in their lives.

Here's the truth: it's great to want to do something well; most people want to be successful. But that's not the same as needing to be perfect.

If you're expecting perfection, you're almost bound to fail, because when it comes to making significant life changes, there's no such thing as perfection. There will be times that you return to your old ways; times you go a little off track. The real trick is not letting those times throw you completely off course. Regain your composure, praise yourself for the progress you have made so far. You really are doing great!

December 26

"It's a new day and a new attitude."

When you throw things away you can expect feelings of guilt to creep in. Why? Because you wonder if you're making a mistake or God forbid you may need it later. The truth is you're not making a mistake and secondly you can be rest assured you won't throw away anything that is essential in your life.

Remember that you are in the process of adopting a new attitude. You don't need clutter in your life. Clutter is a prison wall, an iron fence, a ball and chain, blocking you from the energy you need and that you so much deserve.

It's a new day and the perfect time to set sail with a new attitude. "Clutter Free Forever" is your new mantra!

December 27

"Is laziness holding you back?"

Now, I'm not insuating you're lazy - just by reading this book you're far from it! But think for a moment how your success would be affected if you were more energetic…if moments of tiredness, fatigue, low energy and low motivation weren't part of your daily life. Would you be more successful? How would your life change?

When you look around, it appears that those most successful women seem to have not only a supreme focus, but they also seem to have found a way to beat the "couch potato" gene in all of us. They have retired their excuses and adopted a "do it now" attitude.

There are many ways you can enhance your life by simply "not being lazy." Take some time today to identify some of those ways in your own life.

Once you do you can put the "lazies" behind you and look forward to active and energetic days ahead.

December 28

"Why Not Now?"

You're going to get serious about finding a new job; really you are. You're just going to wait until you win the lotto before you go on vacation. And yes, you honestly want to get in shape and join the gym, but you'll wait until your schedule lightens up. Does any of this sound familiar?

Procrastination can undo even the best of intentions. You've got all these aspirations lined up…you're just waiting, for whatever reason, to get started.

The truth is, procrastination is a vicious cycle.

"I'll do this!" becomes, "I really meant to do this; I'll do it tomorrow for sure." Before you know it, today has turned into tomorrow; those tomorrows have added up and turned into months, sometimes years. And you've made no progress. You're exactly where you've always been.

The good news is that it doesn't have to be this way! You can stop the cycle by taking action.

All you have to do is make a start; you don't have to do everything at once. Take baby steps. Make one phone call; go to the gym one day; take one step toward your goals.

The more you push against your tendencies to procrastinate, the easier it is to break that cycle and go forward. And the faster you can realize your goals!

December 29

"Small victories are worth celebrating."

We're a pretty results-oriented society, so we tend to hold off celebrations until we've reached our final goals. But the truth is that every day holds wonderful successes and important victories. I'm talking about celebrating progress!

Progress can be realizing mini-goals that lead to your ultimate goal or it can even be something more subtle or unexpected, something that happens that has meaning for you. For example, perhaps you were blamed for something at work that was not your fault. Instead of remaining quiet, you confidently stood your ground. Maybe you received a compliment and were surprised by how good it made you feel.

The really wonderful thing about moments like these are that they can happen anytime and sometimes when you least expect

them. They can also turn everything around. Just when you begin
to second guess yourself, you're reminded of your progress.

Don't give up. You are making progress!

December 30

"Adventure is as near as stepping out your front door..."

Too often we think of adventure as this big event that we
have to plan way in advance. We think arrangements must
be made, schedules coordinated, flights booked, time off secured,
etc. With such planning the "adventure" of the adventure is easily
lost.

Adventure is really a decision to do something that inspires
awe, from within. It can be simple, uncomplicated and
spontaneous.

When you're out and about, today, try to look at things in a new
way. Approach your tasks with a fresh sense of curiosity. See
something new, smell something new, touch something new.
Dare to explore and enjoy the experience of living. You will
discover that adventure is easily found in an otherwise ordinary
day.

December 31

"Fuel your resolutions with passion."

While every day is an opportunity for change, New Year's
day is extra special in that regard. It's a time for you to
create new beginnings.

If you have made and broken resolutions in the past and don't
see the point anymore, don't give up! There is something you can
do to secure your success.

Successful "resolvers" create passion. You can too. Passion is
created in two ways. First, your resolution must be your own. If
your resolve is to please someone else, you won't be successful.
Secondly, you must be able to see and feel the results. Visualize

what you'll look like and feel like if you lose weight, quit smoking or make more money.

Whatever you resolve to do this year make it yours, see it and feel it. You'll achieve amazing results simply by infusing your resolutions with passion.

Ordering Information

If you would like to order this book for a friend please visit the
Meditations for Women Web site at:

www.meditationsforwomen.com

This book is not available in bookstores.

Author's Page

Jane Powell is the founder of the Meditations for Women Web site. A popular site specializing in personal development and self-growth tools for women.

- ❖ Free One-Minute Meditations
- ❖ Lively On-Line Community
- ❖ Library of Articles
- ❖ 21 Self-Improvement Programs

For more information visit her Web site at:
www.meditationsforwomen.com